Comments on other *Amazing Stories* from readers & reviewers

"Tightly written volumes filled with lots of wit and humour about famous and infamous Canadians."
Eric Shackleton, *The Globe and Mail*

"The heightened sense of drama and intrigue, combined with a good dose of human interest is what sets Amazing Stories *apart."*
Pamela Klaffke, *Calgary Herald*

"This is popular history as it should be... For this price, buy two and give one to a friend."
Terry Cook, a reader from Ottawa, on **Rebel Women**

"Glasner creates the moment of the explosion itself in graphic detail...she builds detail upon gruesome detail to create a convincingly authentic picture."
Peggy McKinnon, *The Sunday Herald,* on **The Halifax Explosion**

"It was wonderful...I found I could not put it down. I was sorry when it was completed."
Dorothy F. from Manitoba on **Marie-Anne Lagimodière**

"Stories are rich in description, and bristle with a clever, stylish realness."
Mark Weber, *Central Alberta Advisor,* on **Ghost Town Stories II**

"A compelling read. Bertin...has selected only the most intriguing tales, which she narrates with a wealth of detail."
Joyce Glasner, *New Brunswick Reader,* on **Strange Events**

"The resulting book is one readers will want to share with all the women in their lives."
Lynn Martel, *Rocky Mountain Outlook,* on **Women Explorers**

LAURA SECORD

AMAZING STORIES

LAURA SECORD
The Heroic Adventures of a Canadian Legend

HISTORY/BIOGRAPHY

by Cheryl MacDonald

PUBLISHED BY ALTITUDE PUBLISHING CANADA LTD.
1500 Railway Avenue, Canmore, Alberta T1W 1P6
www.altitudepublishing.com
1-800-957-6888

Extreme care has been taken to ensure that all information presented in
this book is accurate and up to date. Neither the author nor the
publisher can be held responsible for any errors.

Publisher	Stephen Hutchings
Associate Publisher	Kara Turner
Series Editor	Jill Foran
Editor	Yvonne Van Ruskenveld

We acknowledge the financial support of the Government
of Canada through the Book Publishing Industry Development
Program (BPIDP) for our publishing activities.

Altitude GreenTree Program
Altitude Publishing will plant twice as many trees as were used
in the manufacturing of this product.

We acknowledge the support of the Canada Council for the Arts which
in 2003 invested $21.7 million in writing and publishing throughout Canada.

Canada Council   Conseil des Arts
for the Arts   du Canada

National Library of Canada Cataloguing in Publication Data

MacDonald, Cheryl, 1952-
Laura Secord / Cheryl MacDonald.

(Amazing stories)
ISBN 1-55439-016-8

1. Secord, Laura, 1775-1868. 2. Canada--History--War of 1812.
I. Title. II. Series: Amazing stories (Canmore, Alta.)

FC443.S4M33 2005   971.03'4'092   C2004-906271-9

An application for the trademark for Amazing Stories™
has been made and the registered trademark is pending.

Printed and bound in Canada by Friesens
2 4 6 8 9 7 5 3 1

For Catherine

Almost anything can be accomplished
with courage and persistence

Contents

Prologue

Laura was exhausted. The June day was hot and humid, and she had been travelling since before dawn. Her feet ached, her dress was torn. All she wanted to do was to lie down and sleep.

But she could not. Darkness was falling. It would be insanity to sleep in the woods. Aside from the ever-present mosquitoes, there were other creatures far more threatening — wolves, wildcats, rattlesnakes. And men, armed men, white and red, who might not think twice before firing at a dim figure moving through the forest at twilight.

She stood at the edge of Twelve Mile Creek. The summer heat had lowered the water a little, but it was still too deep and fast to wade. Instead, Laura gingerly climbed onto a log that had been dropped across the creek as a makeshift bridge. Balancing herself with her arms, she slowly put one foot in front of the other, feeling her way in the gathering gloom.

On the other side she paused. Ahead of her was a steep bank and, somewhere beyond it, the stone farmhouse. She had to reach the farmhouse.

Laura took a deep breath, pushed away the longing for her husband and children, and set her jaw. Then she started to climb.

Minutes later, the creek was far below her. Just a little bit farther and she would be there. She plodded on in the dark until, unexpectedly, she saw a fire. Around it, their faces distorted by the flickering light of the flames, was a group of Iroquois warriors.

"By moonlight the scene was terrifying," Laura later wrote. But she kept moving forward. A second or two later, the warriors noticed her.

"They all rose and, with some yells, said 'Woman,' which made me tremble. I cannot express the awful feeling it gave me; but I did not lose my presence of mind. I was determined to persevere."

Chapter 1
Canada Invaded

t 3 a.m. on October 13, 1812, American troops attacked the small Upper Canadian village of Queenston. As muskets and heavier artillery flashed in the cold drizzle, the sound of gunfire carried up and down the river. Six miles away, at Fort George, Major General Isaac Brock, commander of British troops in Upper Canada, dressed hurriedly and rounded up his men. Meanwhile, the residents of Queenston made their own preparations.

Inside their clapboard house, James and Laura Secord could hear the unmistakable sounds of battle. As a sergeant in the Lincoln militia, James knew he would be needed to defend his country. With the enemy so close, though, it seemed dangerous to leave Laura and their five children behind. So, while James prepared to join his comrades-in-arms, Laura gathered up Mary, Charlotte, Harriet, Charles, and Appollonia and hurried away from the village. "The cannon balls were flying around me in every direction," she later wrote. "I left the place during the engagement."

Although she provides no other details, Laura probably turned her animals loose, reasoning they could fend for themselves for the duration of the battle. As she shut the door of her house, she may have prayed silently, hoping that their comfortable home would survive the cannon fire and other enemy depredations. But there would have been little time to mull over the risks to property. Like the other women of the village, as well as the children, the frail, and the elderly, Laura's first thought was to get to safety. For her, that meant St. David's, where the Secords had family. It was far enough from the scene of the battle to offer protection, but close enough for a quick return to Queenston. And there was no doubt in Laura's mind as she hurried along the road to St. David's that she would be returning as soon as possible. There would be injured men — pray God that James would not be among them — and women would be needed to tend to them.

Queenston was a young but thriving village on the Niagara River. After the American Revolution ended, the British had abandoned Fort Niagara and withdrawn to the Canadian side of the river. There they established a community at

The Secord House, Queenston, Ontario

the northern end of Portage Road, the main route used by freight wagons carrying goods around Niagara Falls and the rapids of the Niagara River. Because the falls were impassable and the rapids far too dangerous to attempt, boats from eastern Canada stopped here. Their cargoes were offloaded into sturdy wagons, then, drawn by teams of oxen or horses, the wagons transported the freight overland to the village of Chippawa, five kilometres below the falls.

Robert Hamilton, a canny Scots merchant, was the founder of the community, which was initially called Niagara Landing or, less formally, the Landing. By 1793, it had been renamed Queenston, and Hamilton was one of the richest and most important businessmen in Upper Canada. His enterprises, including a distillery and tannery, provided him with an excellent income, more than enough to build an imposing two-storey stone house on the banks of the Niagara River.

When the War of 1812 began, Queenston had perhaps 20 houses surrounded by gardens and orchards. Separated by the stone walls or snake fences that were typical of the time, the gardens and orchards provided most of the fruits and vegetables the pioneers needed to feed their families. Close to the water was a collection of businesses and a bustling riverside wharf that brought in a huge variety of goods. Some of these goods were consumed locally, but most were shipped to other destinations. Queenston had also become an important transit point for emigrants coming from the United States via Lewiston, New York. The village was a vital link in the chain of small pioneer communities developing across southern Ontario, and since the Niagara River was barely 400 metres wide at this point, it was mere minutes from the American shore. A successful invasion would allow the Americans to control traffic along the river, hampering the flow of supplies to both the military and civilians farther inland.

Right from the beginning of the war, military and civilians alike realized that Queenston could easily become a target. But because of Queenston Heights, many felt the place could be easily defended. The heights are part of the Niagara

Escarpment, a huge rocky ridge rising 100 metres above the river at this point. Twenty metres in from the river was the village, where Laura and James lived, with the escarpment looming high above it. In anticipation of invasion by the Americans, a redan had been built into the side of the escarpment. Shaped liked the point of an arrow, this two-sided military structure housed an 18-pounder, a gun that could lob 18-pound missiles directly at the American shore.

At the beginning of the October 13 invasion, the Americans had been given clear orders: get to the other side of the river and capture the village and Queenston Heights. In the chilly darkness, some 600 of them set out in boats, while hundreds waited, ready to join them a little later. Under normal circumstances, the trip took only a few minutes. However, as soon as the gunners on the Canadian side realized what was happening, they started firing on the Americans, making it nearly impossible for them to land. Some let their boats drift downstream rather than face the onslaught. Others attempted to land, but could make no progress towards the village.

Like most of the invaders, John Wool, an ambitious and athletic 23-year-old infantry captain, realized that the redan had to be captured if the Americans were to have any hope of victory. It seemed an impossible task, but Wool knew of an overgrown path used by fishermen. Although already wounded in the buttocks, he asked for and received permission to lead a group of 60 men through the bushes in an attempt to capture the redan.

Wool's party found the path, a treacherously steep route leading about 90 metres straight up the side of the escarpment. Undaunted, they struggled upward, hanging onto rocks and bushes as they made the dangerous ascent. As they approached the redan, they saw that only a handful of soldiers had been stationed there. They also saw that the defenders were having a devastating effect on the Americans below, picking them off as they landed on the shore. Many of the invaders huddled under the escarpment, unable to proceed further. Meanwhile, a number of American militiamen surrendered, believing they would be paroled and allowed to return home.

Wool's men attacked the redan, forcing the British to abandon their position. But, just before they retreated, the British soldiers managed to spike the gun, driving a rod into the touch hole and then breaking it off so it could not be fired. The sabotage of the gun was a minor blow for the Americans. With the redan in their hands, it seemed the tide of battle would shift in their favour.

But they still had to reckon with Isaac Brock, unquestionably the most famous military man in Canada at the time. Brock, who had celebrated his 43rd birthday a week earlier, was blond, blue-eyed, and 185 centimetres tall. He was a large man by the standards of the day, an imposing figure who drew attention wherever he went. A skilled horseman, urbane and sociable, Brock also had a deep understanding of human nature. He had the common touch, which made him admired, even loved, by the men he commanded.

In 1812 when the war broke out, Francis Gore, the lieutenant-governor of Upper Canada, was on leave in England. Brock took over his duties, serving as "president" and administrator of the colonial government, as well as head of the military. As war clouds gathered, he found himself frustrated by a lack of cooperation from the legislature and lack of confidence on the part of the general public. On July 29, 1812, barely six weeks after the war began, he informed military head-quarters in Montreal, "My situation is most critical, not from anything the enemy can do, but from the disposition of the people — the population, believe me, is essentially bad — A full belief possesses them all that this Province must inevitably succumb."

Two weeks earlier, American forces under General William Hull had invaded Upper Canada near the Detroit frontier. Hull issued a proclamation promising to protect anyone who remained peaceably at home but also warning that there would be dire consequences if Native warriors participated in the hostilities:

> *If the barbarous and Savage policy of Great Britain be pursued, and the savages are let loose to murder our Citizens and butcher our women and children, this war will be a war of extermination.*

The first stroke with the Tomahawk, the first attempt with the Scalping Knife will be the Signal for one indiscriminate scene of desolation. No white man found fighting by the Side of an Indian will be taken prisoner. Instant destruction will be his Lot.

In the wake of the invasion of Detroit, many members of the militia deserted. Brock issued a proclamation of his own. In it, he tried to convince Upper Canadians that Hull's invitation to accept the protection of the United States was an insult and stressed the economic benefits of ties with Great Britain. He also argued that Natives had as much right to defend themselves as white settlers, especially since so much of their land had been confiscated by Americans. But Brock's proclamation lacked the blunt force of Hull's, and Upper Canadians were not reassured. In fact, according to Brock, the legislators, magistrates, and militia officers of Upper Canada were "sluggish and indifferent." In his assessment, that indifference allowed American sympathizers to do whatever they wanted.

Brock may have been exaggerating somewhat in order to convince his superiors that a stronger military presence was necessary, but there were certainly problems in the colonial administration, as well as in the militia. Upper Canada's citizen-soldiers, like their American counterparts, were generally willing to defend their homes, laying down their lives in the process if necessary. But they saw no good reason to travel far from their families, homes, and farms to defend the province. In some places, members of the militia ignored the call to arms or answered it and then deserted. While Brock could have avoided any real attempt to save the colony, simply gone through the motions and blamed any defeats on the lethargy of the population, such behaviour was alien to his nature. Others might sink into despair, but not Isaac Brock. "Most of the people have lost all confidence," he reported. "I however speak loud and look big."

Both his confidence and his ability to bluff resulted in a military victory early in the War of 1812. On August 16, 1812, he led 1000 men to Fort Detroit. Only 300 were regular troops, but they were accompanied by several hundred Native warriors under the Shawnee chief Tecumseh.

After firing a few shots, Brock demanded that General Hull surrender the fort. If he did not, Brock suggested to the veteran of the American Revolution that his Native allies would "be beyond control the moment the contest commences." Hull surrendered. In addition to more than 200 prisoners, Brock captured needed supplies and ammunition. When news of the bloodless victory reached London, Brock was granted a knighthood. Before news of that honour reached him, the Americans attacked Queenston.

When Brock arrived at the Battle of Queenston Heights, he assessed the situation and sent to Fort George and Chippawa for reinforcements. Then he withdrew to the garden of Robert Hamilton's house to wait for their arrival while defending the village. The choice of location was a logical one, as the front of Hamilton's house faced the village while the back overlooked the river, the American shore, and the enemy gathered there.

Isaac Brock, however, had never been known for his patience, and he quickly grew tired of waiting for reinforcements. American possession of the redan meant more than an end to the deadly fire aimed at the invading troops. In Brock's opinion, it meant that Queenston Heights had fallen to the enemy — and the heights were critical to the defence of the Niagara Peninsula. He would not let them remain in American hands any longer than necessary.

Rallying about 200 men, Brock prepared to tackle the escarpment. "Follow me, boys," he called as he raced his horse Alfred towards the heights. As they neared the escarpment, he stopped in the shelter of a stone wall. "Take a breath, boys," he told his men. "You will need it in a few moments." The men cheered and moments later followed him up the escarpment. Brock's strength of character and charisma were such that men would have followed him into hell if he had asked.

He was clearly visible as he charged up Queenston Heights, a tall, strong man wearing a red tunic, a cocked hat, and a sash presented to him by his Native ally Tecumseh. Sword flashing, he led the men up the escarpment. Then an

American rifleman stepped forward, took careful aim, and fired. Brock fell to the ground, shot through the chest.

George Jarvis, a 15-year-old volunteer with the Light Company of the 49th Regiment, was only a few feet from Brock. "Are you much hurt, sir?" he asked. Brock put his hand on his chest, but said nothing. Isaac Brock, the saviour of Upper Canada, was dead.

Brock's body was carried off the field and hidden in one of the houses in the village. The battle raged on, filling the air with the noise of flying cannonballs and bullets, the clang of swords, the frenzied shouting of men, and the moans of the wounded and dying. Around noon, there was a lull in the fighting. Some American soldiers took the opportunity to rampage through the village, stealing whatever they could carry and destroying many other items.

To the British-Canadian troops it appeared Queenston was lost. Then, from the woods beside the village, Native warriors appeared. Among the leaders were John Norton and John Brant, son of the famous Mohawk chief, Joseph Brant. Wielding tomahawks, they whooped loudly, charged towards the Americans, then melted back into the woods.

The presence of the fierce Native warriors struck terror into the hearts of the Americans on both sides of the river. In Upper Canada, settlers generally lived in peace with neighbouring tribes. But this was not the case in the United States, where the expanding population was pushing aggressively into Native territory. In many instances, there was bloodshed on both sides. Some of the Americans also recalled, either from personal experience or from stories repeated afterwards, the role Native allies of the British had played in the American Revolution in attacking pioneer settlements — killing, scalping, taking captives. The prospect of meeting the Natives in combat made their blood run cold.

As the shock of seeing Native warriors spread through the American side, two British guns opened fire from Robert Hamilton's garden. They were close enough to effectively replace the disabled redan gun. Soon, it was evident that none of the American reinforcements could cross the river. They could only watch as the battle drew to a close.

By 3:30 that afternoon, Lieutenant Colonel Winfield Scott, commander of the American battalion, surrendered. Although greatly outnumbered, the British-Canadian forces had won another victory. About 250 Americans were dead or wounded. Another 925 were prisoners — 500 of them militiamen who had hidden in the woods on the Canadian side rather than engage in battle. British-Canadian losses were minor by comparison — 14 dead, 77 wounded.

Charles Ingersoll, Laura's 16-year-old half-brother, survived unscathed. So did her brother-in-law David, although David's son had been taken prisoner. But there was worse news. Laura's husband, James, was among the wounded. This was hardly surprising. James was a member of a car brigade, a unit charged with transporting large field guns in vehicles drawn by farm horses. The weapons, horses, and wagons made members of the brigade easy-to-recognize targets.

Laura was likely one of several women who walked onto the bloody field when the battle ended. In the fading October sun, the women moved slowly, grimly aware of the mingled smells of gunpowder and blood and the pitiful moans of wounded and dying men and animals. While she searched for James, Laura would have heard other sounds as well — weeping and heartbroken cries of grief as some of her neighbours came upon the bodies of their husbands, sons, and brothers. Shot through the shoulder and knee, James was unable to walk and at risk of dying from blood loss, gangrene, or infection when Laura found him.

One of the legends recounted by Laura's grandson James B. Secord claimed that just as she found James three American soldiers reached him. "Two of them raised their muskets to club him to death. My grandmother rushed in between them, telling them to kill her and spare her husband. One of them spoke very roughly and told her to get out of the way and, shoving her to one side, was about to accomplish this murderous intention. Captain Wool, coming up at that moment, sternly inquired how they dared attempt such a thing."

According to the story, the men were taken into custody, court-martialled, and imprisoned for their actions. Meanwhile, Captain Wool "ordered a party of his men to take Mr. Secord to his own house in Queenston, and did not even make him a prisoner on parole."

Although colourful, the story is mostly fiction. Captain John Wool, the American soldier responsible for capturing the redan gun, was in Queenston having his wounds treated. Laura's own accounts say nothing of three murderous Americans, and by the time she found James, the fighting was apparently over. "After the battle I returned to Queenston," Laura recalled, "and then found that my husband had been wounded; my house plundered and property destroyed." She did note, however, that she was able to get James back to their damaged home "with the assistance of a Gentleman."

Looting happened frequently during the War of 1812, as it has in many other wars. Soldiers, militiamen, and Native warriors all considered enemy property to be fair game, a bonus for their services. Often they stole everything they could carry, including clothing, weaponry, household goods, and food. Sometimes the items were needed for the looters' own comfort or survival, especially if there were food shortages or the looters were far from home and unable to replace clothing or other items. Sometimes, plundering was little more than a free-for-all souvenir hunt. But looting could also become a form of terrorism. Invaders running amok through the homes of enemies might smash furniture or dishes, urinate in flour or other food supplies, kill pigs or dogs, and set fire to buildings. For victims of looters, the loss of personal property was only part of the damage done. The trauma of having enemies invading homes, removing personal items, perhaps threatening or injuring family members, left permanent psychological scars.

Laura had little time to dwell on the damage done to her home. She tended to her husband's wounds as best she could, probably applying herbal remedies to the wounds, wrapping them in clean bandages, and perhaps giving James willow, laudanum, or alcohol for the pain. A bullet would remain in James's knee for the rest of his life. When it was safe to move him, the Secords left Queenston to stay with relatives in nearby St. David's. It would take time to clean up the damage the Americans had caused to the house, and besides, St. David's seemed a safer location. Laura rounded up her children, gathered what belongings she could salvage, and turned her back on Queenston for the time being.

While the residents of Queenston and the surrounding area mourned their losses, it was the death of Isaac Brock that received the most attention. Mingled with grief for a respected public figure was a certain degree of fear. Who would replace Brock? Who would safeguard Upper Canada?

Those questions were being asked as funeral arrangements were made for Brock. His body was retrieved from Queenston and taken to Niagara, where it lay in state at Government House. His aide-de-camp, John Macdonell, had also succumbed to wounds suffered at Queenston. Macdonell, the 27-year-old attorney general of Upper Canada, had tried to recapture the redan after Brock had fallen and had paid for his efforts with his life. Military authorities decided the two soldiers would be buried together.

The funeral began at 10 a.m. on Friday, October 16.

James Secord was still too badly injured to attend, and Laura probably would not have wanted to be far from his side. But some of their family and friends must have attended and related what they had seen. Soldiers from the regular army, members of the militia, and Native warriors lined both sides of the road between Government House and Fort George. Officers had tied black crepe to their swords and donned black arm bands, which they would continue to wear for a month.

The cortege moved slowly to the beat of muffled drums and the sound of two 19-pound guns firing every minute. Included in the long procession was Brock's horse, led by four grooms. Brock's personal servants followed, along with a few other acquaintances. Then came the coffins, each drawn on its own caisson. Macdonell's was the first, followed by Brock's, which was surrounded by nine pallbearers and followed by a number of official mourners, personal friends, and members of the general public. Thousands had turned out to see the general laid to rest.

Captain John Glegg, one of Brock's aides-de-camp, was in charge of the funeral arrangements. He provided the inscription for the plate that was affixed to Brock's coffin:

Here lie the earthly remains of a brave and virtuous Hero, Major General Sir Isaac Brock, Commanding the British Forces, and President Administering the Government of Upper Canada, who fell when gloriously engaging the enemies of his Country at the head of the Flank Companies of the 49th Regiment in the Town of Queenston, on the morning of the 13th October 1812.

The two coffins were placed side by side in the newly built bastion in the northeast corner of the fort as the sound of a 21-gun salute reverberated over the river.

A few weeks later, Native allies, including members of the Six Nations Iroquois, Huron, Chippawa, and Potawatomie, gathered at Fort George to formally express their condolences to their British-Canadian comrades-in-arms. One of them, Chief Kodeaneyonte, presented eight strings of white wampum to Major General Roger Sheaffe, Brock's replacement, as well as to Sheaffe's staff. The wampum, they were told, was meant to wipe away their tears. The chief also produced a large belt of white wampum, which, he assured the British, would guarantee that Brock's grave "would receive no injury." The promise turned out to be something of a prophesy. The graves did remain undisturbed — at least for a little while. But Brock was eventually exhumed and what happened afterward would involve Laura Secord.

Chapter 2
A Question
of Loyalty

L aura and James Secord were victims of a war that had its roots far from their home in Queenston. The War of 1812 began as a result of a long-running struggle between Britain and France. Napoleon Bonaparte was pushing across Europe, trying to create an empire that rivalled that of Rome. Meanwhile, the English were determined to stop him at any cost. Because the United States was sympathetic to France, the British frequently boarded American vessels on the high seas, looking for French citizens or evidence of any kind of aid to the French. And because the British navy was always in need of manpower, American citizens were sometimes seized and drafted into naval service.

Compared to France and England, the United States

was a minor power, little more than a collection of far-flung settlements perched on the edge of a vast wilderness. But Americans had strong ideas about liberty and tyranny, and as far as they were concerned, Britain's wartime practices were just as tyrannical as those that had led to the American Revolution in 1776. On June 18, 1812, American president James Madison declared war on Britain.

Aside from the British navy, the main target for American hostility was British North America, the collection of colonies that had remained loyal to Britain at the time of the Revolution. Of particular interest was Upper Canada, where there were large tracts of rich land, much of it already cleared for farming and settlement. There was also a feeling that Upper Canadians would welcome invaders with open arms. In the words of Thomas Jefferson, conquering Canada was "a mere matter of marching."

A large portion of the population of Upper Canada had roots in the United States. Thousands had fled their homes at the time of the Revolution. Some were driven out by neighbours because of their support of the British. Others deliberately chose to abandon the new United States because they could not support a revolutionary government. They fled to British territory, in many cases leaving behind thriving farms that had been in their family for generations.

James Secord's parents were among these early refugees. When the American Revolution erupted in 1776, James Secord Sr. remained loyal to the British side. A year later he joined Butler's Rangers, a group of Loyalist volunteers who fought against the American rebels and their sympathizers. A short time afterwards, he led a group of 54 neighbours, including his older sons, 22-year-old Solomon, 20-year-old Stephen, and 18-year-old David, to the British garrison at Niagara, where refugee Loyalists were gathering for safety. Among them were many women and children, including James's wife, Madeleine, who arrived in a wagon with her younger children and few possessions other than the clothes they wore. James Sr. joined the Indian Department, working alongside Britain's Native allies, while David remained with Butler's Rangers until they were disbanded in 1784.

At the fort, the Loyalist families were given food, additional clothing, and tents. For the next several months they led a hand-to-mouth existence. Slowly, though, they acquired land and began putting down roots. By August 1782, James Sr. had settled on the Canadian side of the Niagara River. According to a census conducted that month, James had cleared 8 hectares of land and owned 3 horses, 3 cattle, 11 sheep, and 3 hogs. In addition, his stores included 7 bushels of wheat, 100 bushels of corn, and 30 bushels of potatoes.

James Sr. died in 1784, but most of his family remained in the Niagara area. Following the war, many of the men who had served with Butler's Rangers received large grants of land. David acquired 243 hectares at Four Mile Creek, west of Queenston. Another relative, Peter Secord, had built a grist-mill on the creek in 1789. In 1791, David built a sawmill there, laying the foundation for his future prosperity. Soon Four Mile Creek was named St. David's in his honour.

As the son of a Loyalist, James Jr. also received an 81-hectare farm, which was located close to his brother's. Like most young men of the period, he joined the Lincoln militia, attaining the rank of captain before he resigned to concentrate on other interests. James wanted something more than a life as a farmer, and in 1797 he went into business as a merchant. He was 22 and relatively inexperienced, but he was guided by older family members, notably his 36-year-old brother-in-law, Richard Cartwright.

Cartwright, who was married to James's sister Magdalen, had been forced to leave New York because of his loyalist sympathies and had settled in Kingston. He and his business partners — among them Queenston merchant Robert Hamilton — were involved in many different business ventures, including the supplying of goods to British troops in Upper Canada. Aside from his stores, Cartwright also operated mills, a distillery, a tavern, and a shipyard. His work put him in contact with some of the most powerful merchants in Canada, including the McGill brothers of Montreal. He also held a number of prominent positions, serving as a militia officer and judge. In 1792, he was appointed to the legislative council of Upper Canada.

An astute businessman, Cartwright provided goods, contacts, and brotherly advice to young James Secord. With such a powerful man on his side, James seemed to have every chance for success in business.

Around the same time that James went into business, he married Laura Ingersoll. She was 20, a petite, delicate-looking woman with a fair complexion and dark hair. Like James, she was born in the United States. However, Laura was not of Loyalist stock, and the marriage may have shocked some of the more conservative members of the Secords' social circle.

Laura's father, Thomas Ingersoll, was born in Westfield, Massachusetts, in 1749, but in 1774 moved to Great Barrington. He married 17-year-old Elizabeth Dewey, also from Westfield, on February 28, 1775. Laura, the oldest of their four daughters, was born seven months later, on September 13, 1775. (Some of her descendants, noting her early arrival, would claim she was actually born in December.) Thomas and Elizabeth later had three other daughters, Elizabeth, Mira, and Abigail.

A few months after Laura was born, the American Revolution began. Massachusetts was one of the areas where feeling against the British ran particularly high, so it is hardly surprising that Thomas joined the American patriots. By the end of the war, he had risen to the rank of captain. After the war, his involvement in other military activities led to another promotion, and Thomas became a major.

While there must have been some satisfaction in the American victory against the British, the Ingersoll family experienced its share of tragedy during the war years. On February 20, 1784, shortly after the war ended, Elizabeth died. The following year, Thomas married a widow, Mercy Smith, who became stepmother to his four young girls. She and Thomas had no children of their own, and in May 1789, eight days before their fourth wedding anniversary, Mercy died. That September, Thomas married a third time.

Thomas's quick remarriage was not unusual. In colonial times, the household was where most of a family's items were made. Women's work was vitally important to a family's survival. Aside from cooking, cleaning, and caring for children, pioneer women tended fruit orchards and vegetable and herb gardens, raised chickens, milked cows, churned cream into butter, spun and wove cloth, preserved food for winter months, and handled dozens of other tasks. Even women who were wealthy enough to afford a servant or two usually worked right alongside them. Women were often involved in the business world as well, assisting their trades-men-husbands in their shops, or handling sales of goods or property on their behalf. In colonial times, a widower was not only emotionally bereft, he was financially handicapped. For these reasons, many widowers remarried quickly.

Thomas Ingersoll's third wife was another widow, Sarah Whiting Backus. Together they produced seven children, four boys and three girls. The oldest was Charles Ingersoll, born at Great Barrington in 1791.

Laura was 14 when Thomas married Sarah. By the standards of the day she was a young woman, just three years younger than her own mother had been when she married.

Little is known about her life in Great Barrington, but like most young women of the time she must have worked around the house, caring for her younger sisters and her half-brothers and half-sisters as they arrived. She may also have worked in a neighbour's household, a typical practice of the day. By the time she was 20, she would have mastered most of the skills necessary to run her own household.

Whether she had boyfriends in Great Barrington is unknown, but if she had fallen in love, she probably would have stayed behind when her father decided to move to Upper Canada. She did not.

The first settlers in Upper Canada were those who had fought on the side of the British in the American Revolution. In 1789, Lord Dorchester, governor-in-chief of British North America, proclaimed that these people and their descendants would have the right to add "UE" to their names, in recognition of their part in ensuring "Unity of Empire." Eventually, they would be called United Empire Loyalists.

However, the Loyalists who settled in Upper Canada were scattered along a very long, narrow frontier. John Graves Simcoe, the first lieutenant-governor of the province, recognized that more settlers would be required to make the colony flourish. He also reasoned that settlers would be willing to defend their own land against any invaders. So he invited Americans to move to Upper Canada.

In many ways the invitation made sense. The American

Revolution had split families, with some members remaining in the new United States while others emigrated to Upper Canada. Simcoe's invitation allowed some of these families to reunite. Some who had chosen to remain behind in the United States quickly found themselves disillusioned with the new republican government and were happy to move back into the sphere of British influence. Most importantly, many Americans were experienced farmers who had a far better idea of the challenges involved in taming the Canadian wilderness than immigrants from the British Isles or Europe.

However, Simcoe's decision to invite former enemies to settle in Upper Canada was not popular in all quarters. Some established settlers resented the idea of offering land to these people. Although American settlers were required to take an oath declaring loyalty to the King of England, they were still regarded with distrust by many of their neighbours. In spite of the oath, these so-called "late Loyalists" may not have been loyal at all — at least not in the sense of being loyal to the British Crown and British institutions. Recognizing this, some government officials suspected the politics of these new arrivals, convinced that they would create dissension in the colony with their democratic ideas.

Just the same, thousands of Americans chose to move to Upper Canada, willing to put up with suspicion and prejudice because of the opportunities the colony offered. The biggest lure, of course, was land. There was plenty of it at relatively cheap prices. With land, hard work, and a bit of luck, any settler had the chance to prosper and create a legacy that would help sustain his family for generations to come.

To obtain this land, settlers usually submitted petitions to government officials, who considered each request on its own merits. In the case of Loyalists, these petitions usually followed a standard format. Typically, they focused on military service and hardship, including loss of land and possessions, physical injuries, and imprisonment.

There was no guarantee that a petitioner would get the amount of land he wanted in the location he preferred. Someone else might have beaten him to the punch. In addition, many colonists were not above planting seeds of doubt about their fellow petitioners, claiming they had sided with the Americans or were otherwise undeserving. Therefore, petitions for land grants (or other favours, such as appointment to government offices) became exercises in public relations — attempts to convince authorities that your case was more deserving than that of other petitioners.

Further complicating matters was the fact that the Upper Canadian government was not particularly well run. Patronage and corruption were rampant. There was much confusion about who had the authority to approve petitions. As a result, some settlers were promised land by one official, then turned down by another.

Many settlers who came to Upper Canada with high hopes were swiftly disillusioned as their petitions were turned down, the amount of land they felt they deserved was reduced, or others acquired the land on which they had set their sights. Most settlers probably adjusted, but others were embittered by the delays and disappointments. Their bitterness coloured their relationships with both their neighbours and the government, and in some cases, persuaded them that they might have been better off living under the American flag.

Laura's father, Thomas Ingersoll, was one of the "late Loyalists" who ran into difficulties when he tried to settle in Upper Canada. Having fought on the American side during the Revolution, he could make no claim to loyalty or service rendered to the British Crown. Instead, he was one of several enterprising Americans who acquired land in exchange for future services. In 1793, with four associates, he promised to bring a minimum of 40 families to what is now the Ingersoll area, not far from London, Ontario. Each family would receive 81 hectares at a nominal cost, but all were required to make improvements to the property within a specific period of time. Thomas himself was granted 486 hectares, providing he brought in the promised number of settlers, cleared some land, and established a house. Around 1795, he brought his family to the Queenston area, living there until his township was surveyed. In the meantime, he ran a tavern.

Inns and taverns were a vital part of colonial life. Frequently they were little more than private houses, with a room or two made available for travellers needing a place to stay and perhaps another room where they could eat and drink. They served as public gathering places, sometimes doubling as churches, courthouses, or government offices until more suitable buildings were available. And usually they were family enterprises. It is likely that Laura and other family members helped out in Thomas's tavern. There would have been meals to cook and serve, beds to make, linens to wash, and supplies to procure. Whiskey, of course, had to be purchased from a licensed distiller, but the Ingersoll women may have helped make cider, both hard and soft. And, since early taverns were basically extensions of the family home, Laura and her sisters would have dealt directly with visitors, including new immigrants to Upper Canada, travelling businessmen, and government officials.

Business took Thomas away from Queenston from time to time. Along with trying to persuade his fellow Americans to move to Upper Canada, he had to start improvements on his own property. He did manage to clear a bit of land and build a small house. However, the settlers he had promised never materialized, and some of his partners failed to hold up their end of the business arrangement. According to one tradition, the government withdrew Thomas's land grant when officials learned that he had fought with the American patriots during the Revolution. Although this is possible, it is improbable. Thomas had never made any claim to being a United Empire Loyalist. More likely, he lost his grant because he failed to fulfill the terms of his bargain with the government.

Some settlers might have gone back home at this point.

Thomas did not. He moved to the Credit River, about 16 kilometres west of the provincial capital at York (Toronto). There he operated an inn, Government House, which was conveniently located for judges and other government officials travelling on business to the Niagara area or western parts of Upper Canada. Assisted by his wife and younger children, he ran the inn until his death in 1812.

Laura did not move to the Credit River. She was 20 when she arrived in Queenston and was probably the "Miss Ingersoll" mentioned in a list of belles of the period. There were always social functions going on — dances, house parties, outdoor events. And the town was small enough that people who stayed for any length of time got to know most of the other residents. Laura soon met James, and around 1797 they married.

As the date for Laura's marriage approached, she may have experienced a mixture of anticipation and fear. James was from a good family, one that was already well established in Niagara society. The Secords were widely respected, and Laura realized that her marriage to James would probably remove the taint of suspicion that had made her father's life in Upper Canada so difficult. In addition, James was ambitious, eager to follow in the footsteps of his brother and brother-in-law and build a prosperous life for himself and Laura. As they dreamed of their future together, they considered all the little luxuries that would one day be theirs — a fine house of stone or brick, servants, beautiful furnishings, and money to spare.

But first there would be plenty of hard work. Laura understood this. She was luckier than many young women because she was able to afford small indulgences, like lace and other finery. But she still knew what it was to work hard — to churn butter until her arm ached or stitch clothing and household linens until her eyes burned. As a single woman, she had been a helper in her stepmother's household. Now she would be mistress of her own, responsible for every aspect of its operation, including the care of the children who would inevitably arrive. Children, Laura knew, could be a blessing. But there was pain and danger involved in bringing them into the world. Laura hoped she would be strong enough and lucky enough to survive the ordeal of childbirth.

There is some uncertainty about the date or circumstances of the wedding. In the early years of the colony, clergymen were scarce, so many couples went instead to a justice of the peace, who was empowered to perform marriages. Laura and James were probably married by James's older brother David, who by this time was a justice of the peace. However, any records of the wedding that David would have kept were lost when his home was destroyed during the War of 1812. What is fairly certain, given the comparative wealth and influence of the Secords' extended family, is that the wedding was followed by a joyful celebration with many gifts and good wishes bestowed upon the newlyweds.

James and Laura lived in St. David's, where they seemed well on their way to becoming rich and influential members of Niagara society. With an older brother who was already well established as a farmer, businessman, and government official, and a brother-in-law who was one of the most successful entrepreneurs in the colony, James Secord had every chance of building a successful life for himself and Laura. Aside from land, one of the main attractions that drew people to Upper Canada during this period was the great potential for upward mobility. As a frontier society, the colony was just taking shape.

Like many frontier communities, it had no established hierarchy at first. That is not to say that the earliest settlers were more or less on an equal footing. Some brought considerable wealth with them. Others had forged important alliances with powerful figures elsewhere in the colony or beyond. Still others had the advantages of a good education or professional skills. But nearly all of them were refugees, whether political or economic, and they were all starting over in a community where the rungs on the social ladder were empty. Along with scrambling for land, they scrambled for status. They did this by starting businesses, which they expected to grow by leaps and bounds as more people flooded into the colony. In addition, all kinds of government offices needed to be filled. Ambitious individuals who were willing to take some financial risks or work on making connections with the right people could rise from humble beginnings to positions of wealth and importance.

James did experience some degree of success, although

he seems to have taken greater risks than his brother-in-law Richard thought advisable. In 1798, just a year after he started his business, James wrote to a creditor to explain why he could not pay him back immediately. James was on his way to York, where he hoped to get some cash, but at the moment, did not even have enough money to pay for passage down the river and across Lake Ontario. Whether his financial problems were a result of overextending himself or of advancing credit — against Richard Cartwright's advice — is hard to say. One of the problems with running a business in early Upper Canada was that so many of the residents were land-rich and cash-poor. Furthermore, because there was a limited amount of currency circulating in the province, merchants often had to accept payment in goods, such as butter or eggs. Although Cartwright told James it was more profitable in the long run to have goods unsold in the store than to extend credit, James may have had other ideas.

Some of those ideas may have seemed a little too ambitious to those around him. In 1799, James was thinking of establishing a potashery. By leaching wood ash in iron pots, then evaporating the liquid, he could make potash, which was used in fertilizers and some manufacturing processes. Writing to James and Andrew McGill, prominent Montreal businessmen, Richard Cartwright mentioned James's idea and told his business associates that James was honest and hard-working. However, he did have some misgivings about his young brother-in-law's business ability. Cartwright was also concerned about the debt James was running up. Not only did James owe Cartwright money, he also owed the McGill brothers. Cartwright repeatedly reminded James that he needed to pay off that debt. Finally, in 1801, James mortgaged his St. David's farm to his brother-in-law in order to pay off the money he owed his creditors.

Laura may have played a part in creating James's financial problems. Like most women of the period, she probably helped run the business by helping out with various tasks whenever she could and discussing business decisions with her husband. She also shouldered all of James's household responsibilities when he was away on business. And sometimes those responsibilities could be dangerous.

One family story tells of an incident that probably occurred before the war. James had received a large sum of money and word had got around. One night, when Laura was alone with her children and her Black servants, Bob and Fan, a "desperate character" knocked on the door. Laura refused to let him in, and the man replied that he would come in if he wanted to. Thinking quickly, Laura spoke in an Irish accent in an attempt to convince him that more adults were present than actually were. She threatened to set the dog on him, and had Bob growl like a dog, "which it seems he could do to perfection." The stranger went away, reconsidered, and then returned. This time, Laura was waiting with a horse pistol and warned him that if he did not leave she would shoot. Although he continued to threaten that he would get into the house if he wanted to, he finally left.

Laura may also have been just as ambitious as James, and, given her father's early pro-American sympathies, likely felt that she had something to prove to the Niagara establishment. Because she was a gregarious, sociable woman, one way she may have tried to reinforce her family's status in the community was by a conspicuous display of wealth. Recalling her adolescence, one of Laura's daughters remembered that whenever she and her sisters went to fancy balls, their mother insisted that their slippers be dyed the same colour as their ball gowns. This was considered quite an extravagance at the time. It also suggests that Laura and James lived beyond their means, perhaps in an effort to create an impression that James's business was more successful than it actually was.

Money troubles may have inspired Laura and James to move. Around 1801, they left St. David's for a frame house close to Queenston Heights. Queenston was a more important business centre than St. David's so in all likelihood Laura and James believed that they would have better business opportunities there. Over the next several years, James continued to sell goods, including potash, and by 1812, he said in a letter, he was "in easy circumstances." The house was comfortable, and he and Laura had two servants. They had also acquired several pieces of property, which they expected they could eventually sell for a tidy profit. After a rather rocky start, the future looked bright for the Secords and their young family, which by this time included four girls and a boy. Mary, the eldest, was 12, while baby Appollonia was just a year old.

And then the war began. Laura and James likely had mixed reactions to the eruption of hostilities. As Richard Cartwright could testify, wartime could bring profits to some businesses. However, from older members of their family and the community, Laura and James would have known about the depredations of the American Revolution. In some ways, the War of 1812 repeated conditions of the Revolution, when neighbour was turned against neighbour. Because there was such a range of political and personal opinions in Upper Canada, there was plenty of opportunity for conflict. Furthermore, the jockeying for social status and the competition for valuable land had left its mark. Unscrupulous individuals, or those who were merely careless, could drop a word or two in the right ear and instantly a neighbour would be suspected of sympathizing with the enemy or worse forms of disloyalty.

Laura had been in Upper Canada for many years at this point, but memories were long. Despite the undisputed loyalty of the Secord family, the Ingersolls might still have been looked on with a little suspicion. What their personal views were is unknown. Laura might have resented her father's treatment by government authorities, although his success at running a tavern suggests Thomas had little cause for complaint. Both Laura and James might have seen flaws in the way the government was run, and possibly agreed that the more participatory style of government used in the United States would benefit Upper Canadians. But they must also have thought about their day-to-day existence. The most important thing was to survive, keep their family safe, and preserve what they had struggled so hard to earn. Those reasons, perhaps more than anything else, may have motivated Laura to carry a vital message that would influence the outcome of the war.

Chapter 3
Mrs. Secord Takes a Walk

The spring of 1813 brought the war to the Niagara Peninsula with a vengeance. On May 27, under cover of fire from Fort Niagara, the American fleet crossed to the Canadian side of the Niagara River and attacked Fort George. Under the leadership of Lieutenant Colonel Winfield Scott, the Americans inflicted severe damage on the British and Canadians — 50 killed in action, another 300 wounded or missing. To prevent a complete bloodbath, British Brigadier General John Vincent ordered his men to spike the guns, destroy whatever ammunition they could not carry, and abandon the fort. Then he marched them 29 kilometres southwest to John DeCew's house at Beaver Dams.

The next day, Vincent told the militia to return to their

homes. The remainder of the troops withdrew to Burlington Heights, close to the present site of Dundurn Castle in Hamilton.

By occupying Fort George, the Americans had a head-quarters from which to launch attacks on British troops. They also had a spot from which to send out parties to patrol the countryside, making sure the civilian population did not pose any threat.

The occupation of the Niagara frontier, as well as other events in the province, was depressing news for the Secords and other colonists. In Niagara, the presence of enemy troops created a number of problems. Some of the Americans were considerate, treating the colonists as respectfully as they might their own countrymen. But others nursed grudges against the British or Upper Canadians, envying the land they held or the prosperity they enjoyed. Thievery was common, as was suspicion of the local people. While women did not engage in combat, they were targets. One reason was that they were often the producers of food, raising chickens and making bread and butter. These items were usually meant for their families, although what was left over could be sold or exchanged for needed goods. But the occupying army needed to be fed, and they saw nothing wrong with helping themselves to the settlers' supplies.

Laura had her own encounters with troops and other troublemakers, but she was able to handle herself. One traditional story centres on three Americans who came to

Laura's house during the war and asked for water. Although the men were polite enough, one of them said, "When we come for good to this country we'll divide the land, and I'll take this here for my share." Laura was so annoyed that she retorted, "You scoundrel, all you will ever get here will be six feet of earth!" After the Americans left, she regretted her angry response because the men could have done considerable damage to her home. A couple of days later, two of the men returned. "You were right about the six feet of earth, missus," one said. The man who had boasted he would claim the Secord home had been killed.

The presence of an occupying army was just one worry for the colonists. There were also concerns about their Native allies. Early in the war, the Six Nations Iroquois and other Native tribes of the British colonies hesitated to join in the fight against the United States. There were a number of reasons, including some feeling that the Natives of Upper Canada had not been treated well by the British, in spite of supporting them during the American Revolution. Many of them preferred to stay out of the conflict, which they saw as none of their business, and they were encouraged to do so by tribes still living in the United States. There were also fears that, should the United States win the war, the Canadian tribes would be punished for any action against the Americans, and once again they would lose their land.

Eventually, though, it became clear to some Natives that their best chance to preserve their territory in Canada was to fight alongside the British. But their presence caused other problems. Some of the settlers had considerable respect for the Natives, remembering how they had fought side by side in the American Revolution, and encouraged them to take up arms. As Brock had pointed out in his response to William Hull's proclamation, "They are men, and have equal rights with all other men to defend themselves and their property when invaded." But others, including the late Loyalists, felt quite differently, remembering the attacks on native settlers during the American Revolution. And there was also General Hull's warning that any white man fighting alongside a Native would be killed instantly.

The Secords and the other colonists of the Niagara area were living in a state of siege, not quite sure whom to trust, constantly worried about their personal safety and that of their neighbours and loved ones. Meanwhile, they were also trying to survive: planting crops, caring for livestock, conducting business as best they could despite the disruptions caused by the war. When men were away, these chores frequently fell to the women, adding to their burdensome household tasks. Laura faced all these problems and more. James was slowly getting better, but it would be many months before he could walk more than a few steps.

Although she had two servants, Laura likely worked alongside them, as did most pioneer wives. While Fan might be expected to handle the heavier tasks, such as filling the huge iron pots with water on wash day, Laura would have supervised and probably washed the more delicate items herself. Similarly, Fan and Laura probably split the cooking chores. In addition, like most pioneer children, the Secord youngsters were expected to help with various chores, both within the household and in James's business. Mary and Charlotte, who were about 12 and 10 at the start of the war, were old enough to handle most domestic duties, while 5-year-old Harriet would have been given lighter tasks, including keeping an eye on baby Apollonia. Meanwhile, Bob, the Secords' male servant, probably handled whatever outdoor chores James could not, undoubtedly assisted by James and Laura's son Charles. Although James considered himself first and foremost a businessman, the Secords, like most families in Upper Canada, grew most of their own food.

How deeply Laura and the rest of the family were involved in James's business is difficult to say, but many businesses of the era were truly family enterprises. Laura may have helped keep accounts and written letters to customers or creditors, while the older children may have run various errands.

Both James and Laura were disheartened by the continuation of the war. By early June, as many as 3500 American troops had moved westward to Stoney Creek, not far from the British headquarters at Burlington Heights. On the night of June 5, the British staged a surprise attack against the Americans. The fight took place in the darkness, much of it in wooded areas, and was extremely confusing. Next day, no one was quite sure who had won the battle. However, the Americans were in retreat, pulling back towards the Niagara Peninsula with the British in hot pursuit. General John Vincent led the chase as far as Forty Mile Creek (Grimsby) then stopped. His decision angered many, who felt that a bit more aggressiveness may well have pushed the Americans back to their own side of the border.

One of those disgusted by Vincent's hesitancy was Captain James FitzGibbon. He felt that something more needed to be done. He was also convinced that he was the man to do it.

James FitzGibbon's confidence in his own ability stemmed from his early experiences. Born in 1780, he was the second son of a poor Irish farmer in Glin, County Limerick. As a teenager, he joined the Knight of Glin's yeomanry corps. Like Canadian militia units, the yeomanry was formed to provide civilian defenders in case of invasion, in this case by the French, who were then at war with Britain. FitzGibbon learned the drills so well that he was quickly promoted to the rank of sergeant.

Members of the yeomanry were not required to serve anywhere but in their home territory. FitzGibbon, however, was hungry for adventure and eventually enlisted in 1799 in the 49th Regiment of Foot, under the command of Isaac Brock. FitzGibbon's first taste of battle came that November at Egmond-aan-Zee, Holland. The day ended badly for the young soldier and several of his comrades-in-arms when they were captured by the French. FitzGibbon remained a prisoner of war until an exchange was arranged in January, but he put the time to good use by learning the language of his captors.

In 1802, the 49th Regiment was posted to Canada. James FitzGibbon did everything he could to rise in the ranks. Like his idol, Isaac Brock, he was frequently impulsive, but he showed enormous initiative. He was also very likeable, tall, good natured, and exceptionally strong.

When the War of 1812 began, it seemed he would have many chances for promotion if he acquitted himself well and won the approval of his superiors. Vincent's reluctance to move past Forty Mile Creek gave him the opportunity he was looking for. FitzGibbon volunteered to take 50 men to DeCew's. There they would root out those who were helping the enemy, stop American raiders from capturing supplies or imprisoning local residents, and provide what intelligence they could to headquarters. His request was quickly approved. With 50 soldiers hand-picked from various companies, he left for Beaver Dams on the night of June 12.

Beaver Dams was a tiny community on a branch of Twelve Mile Creek, south of Thorold. It had taken its name from the beaver dams that were plentiful in the surrounding marshland. John DeCew (the name was also spelled DeCou or DeCow) was the most prominent local citizen. A Loyalist from New Jersey, he had mills and orchards and dealings in various commercial enterprises. By the time the War of 1812 began, he and his wife, Catherine Docksteder, had replaced their log cabin with an impressive two-storey stone house.

DeCew was a commissioned militia officer and during the war commanded a company of the 2nd Lincoln Militia. He was among the volunteers serving at Fort George when the Americans attacked and captured the fort. On his way home from that engagement, he ran into an American patrol and was taken into custody and sent to the United States. After several months in a notorious Philadelphia prison, he escaped in April 1814. Two months later, he was back with his regiment in the Niagara Peninsula.

Before his capture, DeCew had turned part of his house over to the British for use as the local headquarters and supply depot. While Catherine and her children used the upstairs rooms, soldiers occupied the lower floor. The house was strategically located near roads leading north to the community of Twelve Mile Creek, northeast to Queenston, and southeast to Niagara Falls and Chippawa. The creek and the escarpment also provided natural barriers that would slow down any attacking force.

Soon after James FitzGibbon and his soldiers arrived, rumours started to circulate about what was going on in the woods and ravines around the DeCew house. Although trained in formal European military tactics, the men of the 49th Regiment were now practising frontier fighting methods, mastering the guerrilla-type techniques used by both Native warriors and many militiamen on both sides. Sometimes blood-curdling screams could be heard from the woods as FitzGibbon and his men practised their attacks. These activities added to the already fierce reputation of the Green Tigers, the nickname given to members of the 49th Regiment because of the green facings on their scarlet uniforms. When fighting frontier-style, they traded their conspicuous scarlet for green jackets that made them difficult to recognize as soldiers.

Part of the mission assigned to FitzGibbon and his men was to meet American marauders on their own terms. Secure in their occupation of Fort George, a number of American raiders combed the countryside, harassing settlers, stealing food, and capturing able-bodied men who could fight against them. The most notorious of the raiders was Cyrenius Chapin, a New Englander who had become a frontier doctor in the area of Buffalo, New York. Before the war he tended both white and Native patients on both sides of the border, thus acquiring a substantial knowledge of the various roads that ran through the Niagara region. Chapin, who was rabidly loyal to the United States, used that knowledge to root out anyone who posed a threat to his cause. Usually he was accompanied by 50 armed riflemen.

The arrival of FitzGibbon and his Green Tigers hampered Chapin's activities, and there were several clashes between the two groups. One dramatic encounter occurred in late June, at a place called the Crossroads, near what is now the intersection of Lundy's Lane and Portage Road in Niagara Falls.

To avoid drawing unwelcome attention, FitzGibbon stationed his men in the woods nearby while he went ahead to assess the situation. As he approached Deffield's Inn, Mrs. James Kerby, wife of a militia officer, ran out to tell him that Chapin's raiders, along with a company of American soldiers, had just passed by. Meanwhile, FitzGibbon noticed a horse in front of the inn. Suspecting it belonged to one of the raiders, he dismounted and entered the inn, where he immediately found himself staring at a loaded musket.

Thinking quickly, FitzGibbon put out his hand and greeted the American soldier as if he were an old friend. The momentary confusion was all that FitzGibbon needed. He grabbed the barrel of the American's gun and ordered him to surrender.

Then another American rifleman took aim. Again, FitzGibbon managed to grab the gun under his arm. In spite of his unusual strength — which he liked to say he had developed as a boy on his father's farm — there was no telling how long FitzGibbon would be able to hold the two guns. But he was determined. He pushed and pulled the two Americans out of the inn, "swearing and demanding them to surrender."

The Americans fought back. As the men tussled in front of the inn, Mrs. Kerby shouted at two passersby for help. They ignored her. One small boy started throwing stones at the Americans to little effect. Then one of the men released his rifle, pulled FitzGibbon's sword out of its scabbard, and prepared to run the British officer through.

By this time, the innkeeper's wife had appeared, holding her baby in her arms. Barely thinking about the consequences, she ran forward and kicked the sword out of the American's hand. The American bent down to retrieve it, but Mrs. Deffield was quicker. Putting her baby down, she grabbed the sword and ran with it into the inn.

Meanwhile, her husband had emerged from the inn. Deffield helped FitzGibbon subdue the two Americans, who were taken into custody. Word of the tussle spread quickly, amusing many of the Niagara-area residents and deeply embarrassing Chapin and his men. Chapin had already made it clear he wanted the Green Tigers out of the way. Now he made up his mind to persuade military authorities to attack DeCew's house. All he needed was 500 soldiers.

He presented his plan to Lieutenant Colonel Charles Boerstler at Fort George. Boerstler, who considered Chapin a "vain boasting liar," was not impressed. But Chapin persisted and made no attempt to keep his plans secret.

On June 21, a small group of Americans appeared at Laura Secord's door demanding food. Cyrenius Chapin was likely among them. According to a Secord family tradition, Laura told her servants, "Put everything you have got on the table because we cannot resist them." She also provided liquor and stayed nearby as the men ate and talked.

Sometime during the course of the meal, she heard

them discuss plans to attack Beaver Dams. Possibly they boasted about the upcoming attack, trying to instill fear in the Secord household and making it clear that they would put an end to FitzGibbon and his Green Tigers. More likely, the conversation was among the soldiers themselves, who may have paid no attention to Laura as she served them. Accustomed to eating in taverns, the soldiers gave little thought to women who waited on them.

Another version of the story claims that James actually heard the news from an American officer. Given his limited ability to move about, perhaps James overheard the unwelcome visitors discussing the plans. Or perhaps a boastful American deliberately told James the news, realizing that his injury made him powerless to do anything about it. Whoever actually heard the details, James and Laura discussed the threat. They both realized how important it was to warn FitzGibbon. They were tired of the American occupation, sick at the destruction of the countryside and the loss of personal items. There was no question, however, of James taking the message. He still could not walk any distance. Laura would have to warn FitzGibbon herself.

In retrospect, it is not clear whether Laura deliberately set out to take the message to Beaver Dams or was forced by circumstances to make the journey. American troops had withdrawn from Queenston on June 21, the day that the Secords learned of the plan to attack Beaver Dams. But there was no way she could know where else she might encounter regular soldiers or Chapin's raiders. If she was going to make a journey alone, the best time to start would probably be early in the morning, before too many people were on the road.

Later accounts of her journey suggest she deliberately set out to deceive the soldiers by heading for St. David's, instead of going directly to DeCew's house. But Laura may have simply been trying to find someone else to carry the message. St. David's was the logical place to start, as she and James had several relatives there, including Charles Ingersoll, Laura's half-brother.

Charles had been ill with a fever and was staying at the home of Hannah Secord, widow of James's brother Stephen. If he was better, perhaps he could carry the message. If not, Hannah had teenage sons, James and David, who could easily handle the task. In the meantime, Charles's illness gave Laura an excuse for her visit should she encounter unfriendly Americans. Doctors were scarce in pioneer Upper Canada, so women generally took care of their family's health needs, concocting herbal remedies, tending to the sick, bringing children into the world. They shared those duties within their extended family, spelling one another off in times of prolonged sickness. It made perfect sense for Laura to visit Charles, and to help her sister-in-law tend to him or take on some household duties that had inevitably fallen by the wayside.

Early on June 22, Laura set out. It was about 4:30 in the morning, shortly before sunrise. Laura dressed in a print dress, a brown-patterned fabric covered with orange flowers. Like most pioneer women, she would have worn a hat to protect her complexion from the sun and a white kerchief around her neck. On her feet were kid leather slippers, tied at the instep.

As dawn broke, the temperature rose. It had rained the night before, and now the countryside steamed with humidity. It was going to be a hot day, and by the time Laura reached her half-brother, she was already feeling the heat. At Hannah's house, Laura explained her mission. Charles was still too ill to leave his bed. James and David were away with the militia. Laura realized she would have to carry the message herself.

Laura, Hannah, and Charles likely discussed the best way to proceed. Charles probably suggested that Laura go to Shipman's Corners (St. Catharines) and relay her information to William Hamilton Merritt. He and Charles had fought together as cavalrymen at the battle of Queenston Heights with the Niagara Light Dragoons. At the time, Merritt's father, Thomas, was commander. In the ensuing months, however, Thomas had retired and young William was now captain of the unit. Perhaps Charles was worried about Laura's safety if she came too close to FitzGibbon's headquarters at a time when American raiders were particularly angry with the Green Tigers. On the other hand, he may have felt that William Hamilton Merritt, knowing Laura was his sister, would more readily believe her story. There is also the possibility that Charles recognized the impact Laura's news might have on Merritt's career. His friend was ambitious — eventually he would spearhead the building of the Welland Canal and serve as a member of the House of Assembly. Perhaps Charles thought that if Merritt had a part in averting any planned attack at Beaver Dams, he would be rewarded in some manner by provincial authorities. And if Charles was partly responsible for involving Merritt, Merritt might reciprocate by helping Charles advance in his own career. By the end of the discussion, it was decided that, rather than proceeding to Beaver Dams, Laura should head further north, to Shipman's Corners.

When she left Hannah's house, Laura had company. Elizabeth, Hannah's eldest daughter, offered to walk with her. Elizabeth and Charles were engaged, and it is quite possible that the younger woman had a special affection for her future sister-in-law. Despite her own delicate health, she willingly risked the heat and the dangers of the road to accompany Laura.

To minimize the chance of meeting any Americans, the women took a roundabout route, avoiding the main roads between villages. The terrain was rough, covered with high grass and bushes, and the temperature continued to climb as the morning progressed. Elizabeth soon grew weary. By the time they reached Shipman's Corners, she was exhausted, too tired and footsore to continue. Laura was tired, too, but she had no choice but to go on. William Hamilton Merritt was away, and once again it fell to her to carry on with her precious information.

Elizabeth sought shelter with friends, who likely provided Laura with a bit of refreshment before she continued the journey. Again, Laura avoided the well-travelled road between Shipman's Corners and Beaver Dams. Instead, she journeyed cross-country, using Twelve Mile Creek as a guide to her destination.

Laura plodded forward. The sun began to drop, but the heat continued. Her clothing was soaked with sweat, her feet ached, and her eyes blurred from the heat, the humidity, and fatigue. Still she kept moving. Sometimes it seemed she was walking through a dream, nearly lulled to sleep by the temperature and the lazy buzzing of insects in the sun-soaked fields. Then she would shake herself, look around to get her bearings, perhaps stop by the creek for a drink of cool, clear water or to soak her feet. It would be so easy to close her eyes, doze off, just for a moment or two. But Laura would not give in. Her message had to be delivered, and she had already lost too much time.

As the sun set, there was some relief from the heat, but there were other hazards to contend with, including mosquitoes and night-prowling animals. In the darkness, it was more difficult for Laura to see where she was going. She stumbled from time to time, and at one point she lost her shoes in the thick woods.

Still she kept on, crossing the creek on a fallen

tree, scrambling up the steep bank as she approached DeCew's property.

And then she came upon the Native encampment.

They were strong, fierce men, hardened by the physical demands of their way of life and by war. Very little could surprise them, but the sight of a white woman, exhausted and bedraggled, in the middle of the woods, certainly was strange. What was she doing here?

Laura's first reaction was sheer, paralyzing terror. Like most Americans of her generation, she had grown up with tales of Native brutality, savage attacks on pioneer settlements, men butchered and scalped, women violated, children kidnapped. No matter that whites could be just as savage in their attacks on Natives — the horrific images of marauding warriors was deeply ingrained in the colonial psyche. But there was another image, one that Laura was familiar with because of her connection with the Secord family. Native warriors had also fought and died alongside British and Canadian men during the American Revolution and more recent battles. While there was still prejudice, many of those British-Canadians, men like Laura's own father-in-law, spoke admiringly of the warriors' courage, loyalty, and devotion to those they respected.

Laura let that image guide her, along with her determination to accomplish her goal. Trembling and (because the warriors did not understand much English) struggling to make herself understood, she explained her purpose. "I went up to one of the chiefs," she later wrote, "made him under-stand that I had great news for Capt. Fitzgibbon, and that he must let me pass to his camp, or that he and his party would be all taken." There was some hesitation. Was this a trick, a subterfuge? The warriors debated among themselves, dark eyes taking in the travel-soiled figure of the woman before them, tossing out various ideas about where she had come from and why. "The chief at first objected to let me pass, but finally consented, after some hesitation, to go with me and accompany me to Fitzgibbon's station."

The warriors doused their fire, picked up their weap-ons and other belongings. Then, gathering around the small, exhausted woman, they set out across the fields for FitzGibbon's headquarters.

Chapter 4
The Battle of Beaver Dams

amplight reflected warmly in the walnut panelling of the DeCew house when Laura was brought before James FitzGibbon. The tall, muscular soldier with the lively grey eyes was shocked at her condition. "Mrs. Secord was a person of slight and delicate frame, and made the effort in weather excessively warm, and I dreaded at the time that she must suffer in health in consequence of fatigue and anxiety, she having been exposed to danger from the enemy, through whose line of communication she had to pass."

Laura had travelled nearly 32 kilometres since leaving her home in Queenston that morning. FitzGibbon must have offered her a chair and listened quietly to her story, asking the occasional question. "I told him what I had come for and what I had heard," Laura wrote later. "The Americans intended to make an attack upon the troops under his command, and would, from their superior numbers, capture them all."

FitzGibbon thanked Laura for the information and arranged for her to stay at a neighbouring house overnight. As soon as she was safely accommodated, he sent a report to Lieutenant Colonel Cecil Bisshopp, who was stationed at Forty Mile Creek. Major De Haren, who was near Shipman's Corners, was also informed. FitzGibbon asked for reinforcements, which he knew would take some time to reach him. In the meantime, he made other preparations. A little over a mile away were more than 400 Native warriors. On June 21, about 200 had arrived from Lower Canada under the command of Dominique Ducharme. A former fur trader from Lachine, Ducharme was 48 years old and had served with the militia of that region since the beginning of the war. His men were joined by another 200 Native troops from Brantford, led by Captains William Johnson Kerr and John Norton. Kerr, 26, was a grandson of Sir William Johnson, the Irish superintendent of American affairs who had persuaded the Six Nations Iroquois to remain loyal to Britain during the American Revolution. His grandmother was Johnson's Native wife, Molly, whose brother Joseph had led part of the Six Nations to the Brantford area following the Revolution. Kerr himself was a veteran of Queenston Heights, having fought there alongside his cousin John Brant and John Norton.

Laura Secord Meets FitzGibbon, painting by Lorne K. Smith

Norton was probably one of the most colourful individuals among the Native troops. Son of a Scottish woman and a Cherokee man, he had been born and educated in Scotland, served for a time in the British army in North America, and then deserted. Adopted by the Six Nations Iroquois, he was highly respected by many of them, as well as by whites, as a diplomat and warrior. His superior education, leadership skills, and intimate knowledge of white and Native society gave him a prominent place in Upper Canadian society. A few weeks after the battle at Beaver Dams, Norton married his second wife, Catherine. She was 16, Norton close to 50. The match scandalized many and led to tragedy several years later, when Norton killed a former comrade-in-arms who was paying too much attention to Catherine. Norton threw his wife out of their house on the Grand River and turned himself into authorities. Found guilty of manslaughter, Norton was fined £25, which he promptly paid. A short time later, he left Upper Canada forever.

After hearing Laura Secord's news, James FitzGibbon sent out several of his men to guard the approaches to the DeCew house, augmenting their ranks with a large number of Native warriors. While some settled in to wait for the enemy to make a move, others travelled around the countryside, gathering what intelligence they could. On the morning of June 23, Dominique Ducharme took about two dozen of his men to scout around the Niagara River. There was absolutely no sign of troop activity, although they did spot a barge loaded with soldiers. The Natives fired upon the Americans, killing four and taking six prisoners. They were so close to Fort George at this point that the sound of gunfire brought out the American cavalry. As Ducharme's men fled, two young Iroquois stayed behind, hoping to capture American horses. Instead, one of them was taken prisoner.

Laura had slept soundly after her long walk, although it would be some time before she recovered completely from her ordeal. While Ducharme was harassing Americans, she started back to Queenston, this time by a more direct route. "I returned home next day, exhausted and fatigued," she later recorded.

According to Laura's information, the Americans were planning to attack on June 23. But no attack came that day. Perhaps the men she had overheard had got the dates wrong, perhaps they had deliberately misled her. Or perhaps it was simply a case of a delay in issuing orders along the military chain of command.

Meanwhile, Cyrenius Chapin's report to Major General Henry Dearborn had received more careful consideration than Lieutenant Colonel Charles Boerstler had been willing to give it. On June 23, Dearborn ordered Boerstler to take 500 men and attack FitzGibbon's headquarters. They left Fort George at 11 p.m. that night, travelling the 10 kilometres to Queenston as swiftly and silently as possible. Once they arrived in the village, patrols were sent out to prevent the locals from taking word to British-Canadian troops. The American soldiers spent the rest of the night in darkness, under orders not to light so much as a candle. As much as possible, Boerstler wanted the attack to be a surprise. But the American colonel was not the only one planning a surprise.

Back in late May, worried about the turn the war was taking, many Natives had considered withdrawing from the hostilities. Initially, when the British pulled back to Burlington Heights, a few hundred Iroquois from the Grand

River area stayed in the Niagara area. John Norton thought Beaver Dams was a good location to face the Americans. With Lake Ontario and the escarpment hemming them in on two sides, and marshy areas and Twelve Mile Creek hampering movement on another, it would be difficult for them to retreat in a pitched battle. Norton was unable to persuade all of the Grand River warriors to remain, however, and by the time Laura had reached FitzGibbon's headquarters, about 100 of them had drifted back to their homes. But other Natives arrived to support the British.

A large group of warriors were Mohawks from Kahnawake (Caughnawaga, near Montreal), Kanesatake (Oka), and Akwesasne (Cornwall). As well, there were Mississaugas, Ojibways, and warriors from the northwest. These Native fighters spread out over the Niagara area, harassing and killing the Americans whenever they ventured out of Fort George.

Now their goal was to stop the Americans before they reached Beaver Dams. Boerstler had ordered his men to march on FitzGibbon's headquarters early that morning. As they made their way between Queenston and St. David's, two of Dominique Ducharme's Native scouts spotted them. Fearing the scouts would relay the news to FitzGibbon, the Americans fired at them. One of the warriors was killed, but the other escaped and raised the alarm in the Native camp.

Meanwhile, the Americans ran into difficulty. Captain Chapin had bragged that he knew almost every road in the Niagara Peninsula, and he was serving as guide to the

American force as it made its way to Beaver Dams. But shortly after leaving St. David's, Chapin became confused. Exasperated, Boerstler had to ask directions from the locals and pressed one of them into service as a guide.

Ducharme had already asked Major De Haren for permission to hide his men in the woods, rather than assemble them in regular battle formation. De Haren had agreed, and as the Americans made their way from Queenston, the warriors waited patiently for the right moment.

The Americans walked on, not stopping for rest or refreshment. At the front were mounted riflemen, who moved along the ranks, ready to engage the enemy at a moment's notice. They were followed by 300 members of the 14th Infantry. Behind them were two artillery wagons, each drawn by a team of four horses and carrying a 6-pound gun and a 12-pound gun, as well as other ammunition. A little further back were about 100 men of the 6th and 23rd regiments, led by Major Taylor. In the rear were cavalrymen. Altogether, there were nearly 500 American troops.

Having seen the Native scouts near St. David's, Boerstler and his officers realized there was a good chance that FitzGibbon would know of their approach long before they came in sight of DeCew's house. As they neared the British headquarters, they saw a group of red-coated British soldiers. The sound of bugles and muskets made it clear that they were on the alert. There was no chance of surprise now, but Boerstler was not about to turn back.

He marched his men past a stand of beech trees where, unknown to him, 400 Natives were hiding. According to one account, he paused at this point to question some of the Canadians they had captured. Perhaps one of them was the guide they had taken near St. David's. Suddenly, shots rang out. The cavalry charged, but the Native warriors stood their ground, then withdrew into the trees. Major Taylor's horse was shot from under him. Early in the battle, Colonel Boerstler was also wounded.

In the midst of the fighting, someone reported to Boerstler that Captain Chapin, the man who had urged the attack on FitzGibbon's headquarters, was hiding. Boerstler galloped back along the American line and found Chapin hiding near the ammunition wagon, which had been left in a partly sheltered hollow. "For God's sake, do something!" Boerstler shouted. If Chapin would not fight, the least he could do was help distribute ammunition or move the wounded. Half-heartedly, Chapin got a keg of ammunition, mounted his horse, and brought it to one of the American soldiers. Then he headed back for cover near the wagon.

By 11 a.m., the battle had been raging for about three hours. The Americans were near exhaustion, having marched for hours in the June heat without any water or rest. With the sun and humidity adding to their misery, it seemed they could not last much longer. Boerstler was considering a retreat when the Native warriors attacked again.

The Americans had nowhere to go. The woods on one

side were full of hostile warriors. The nearby swamps were treacherous. The creek and the escarpment presented hazards of their own. Any retreat would have to be back in the direction from which they had come. After conferring with his officers, Boerstler rejected that option, estimating that he might lose as many as one-quarter of his men if he attempted a retreat. To make matters worse, ammunition was running low. Boerstler decided to surrender.

The first attempt to surrender was a failure. Captain Ducharme tried to stop the fighting when he understood that Boerstler was ready to give up, but the Native warriors were so caught up in the battle that they paid no attention. At this point, it appeared the Battle of Beaver Dams might turn into a massacre.

James FitzGibbon had been watching the battle from a slight rise a short distance away.

Taking a chance that the Americans had no idea how few men he commanded, FitzGibbon arranged some of his Green Tigers across the road, apparently blocking the Americans' path of retreat. Then, waving a white flag to signal a truce, he led the way towards the fighting.

Boerstler's troops had suffered severe casualties, with about one in five of his men killed or wounded. In theory, there was still a chance for an American victory, but James FitzGibbon was not going to let that happen. He moved towards the Americans while the bugles sounded the ceasefire.

Boerstler sent Captain Andrew McDowell to negotiate. FitzGibbon used the opportunity to delay any resumption of the fighting for as long as possible. He knew reinforcements were on the way, and he realized that if he could keep the Americans talking long enough, the reinforcements might arrive in time to tip the balance in favour of the British-Canadian troops. As he talked to McDowell, he used the same tactic his mentor, Isaac Brock, had employed at Detroit. He informed the American captain that additional Native warriors from the northwest were in the vicinity. If they came upon the Americans, FitzGibbon would not be able to control them.

The Americans had already seen the difficulty Captain Ducharme had experienced in controlling Native troops that morning. McDowell returned to Boerstler with his report. The American officers talked briefly, coming to the conclusion that there would be far less loss of life if they surrendered immediately.

The two sides began to negotiate the terms of surrender. It was agreed there would be no looting, that private property would be respected. American officers could keep their side-arms. Members of the militia and the volunteers would be returned to the United States, providing they agreed not to take up arms again during the war.

The Americans capitulated: 462 soldiers, including 22 officers, surrendered. They were preparing to lay down their arms when Major De Haren arrived with a small body of soldiers. Ignoring FitzGibbon's arrangements, De Haren started to negotiate with Boerstler. FitzGibbon had to remind him that the Americans were already his prisoners. Still determined to exercise his authority, De Haren ordered the Americans to march through the British ranks and place their weapons on the far side. This was perhaps designed as an extra humiliation, a means of forcing the defeated Americans to come face to face with their conquerors. But it might have been disastrous because, as they marched through the British ranks, the Americans would have realized how few in number the British were. Once again, FitzGibbon's quick wit came to the rescue. He pointed out that the Natives might react badly when faced with Americans still carrying arms. Boerstler heard the exchange between the two British officers and demanded that his men be allowed to give up their weapons immediately.

Although he did stop further bloodshed, FitzGibbon was unable to control looting. As the citizens of Niagara had already learned, looting was a standard part of war. When the Americans captured Fort George, the dead British-Canadians were stripped of clothing and all possessions and the town of Niagara was plundered. While the officers at Beaver Dams might promise there would be no such action, the troops had other ideas. The Mohawks from the Grand River demanded goods as reward for their service, including swords, guns, and clothing. And they were not the only ones. One British lieutenant obtained a black horse, complete with saddle and bridle, as well as some pistols in the aftermath of the fighting.

For the Americans, the battle had other repercussions. One of the first consequences was that Major General Henry Dearborn was relieved of his command in Upper Canada. Lieutenant Colonel Charles Boerstler also came under official scrutiny. Following the war, a court of inquiry in Baltimore, Maryland, investigated Boerstler's conduct at the battle. After sifting through all the evidence, the court concluded that he was a "brave, zealous and deliberate officer." The court also praised the conduct of the regular officers and soldiers, implying that the major responsibility for the loss at Beaver Dams lay squarely on the shoulders of American volunteers like Cyrenius Chapin.

The Battle of Beaver Dams was a significant victory, especially for the Native warriors, who had forced the Americans to surrender with virtually no assistance from white troops. As John Norton would later comment, "The Cognawaga Indians fought the battle, the Mohawks or Six Nations got the plunder, and FitzGibbon got the credit." In his official report to Colonel Bisshopp, FitzGibbon stressed the part of Native fighters. "In this affair the Indian warriors under the Command of Captain Kerr were the only Force actually engaged; to them great merit is due, and to them I feel particularly obliged for their gallant conduct on this occasion." However, the general public was not willing to give Native warriors a starring role in what was viewed as an important battle.

In newspaper reports, as well as in the popular imagination, it was James FitzGibbon who emerged as the hero of the moment. The *Montreal Gazette* reported on the victory in glowing terms, praising FitzGibbon for his "cool determination," his "hardy presence of mind," and the brilliant result. William Johnson Kerr would spend several years trying to get official recognition for the part Native warriors had played in the battle. Supporting his efforts, FitzGibbon would write, "With respect to the affair with Captain Boerstler, not a shot was fired on our side by any but the Indians. They beat the American Detachment into a state of Terror, and the only share I claim is the taking advantage of a favourable moment to offer them protection from the Tomahawk and the scalping knife."

The Native warriors were not the only ones whose involvement with the victory went unacknowledged. Despite her heroic walk, there was no mention of the woman who had made the dangerous, exhausting 32-kilometre trip to alert FitzGibbon to the American attack.

Chapter 5
Unsung Heroine

ews of the victory at Beaver Dams spread quickly, but very few people were aware of the part that Laura Secord had played. Obviously, her immediate family knew, including James, her half-brother Charles, and her niece Elizabeth. However, the details of her walk were kept secret, out of concern for the safety of Laura and her family. The outcome of the war was still uncertain, and as long as the Americans posed a threat, the less they knew about Laura's role in their defeat the better.

In December the Americans abandoned Fort George, burning the village of Niagara before they returned to the United States. British forces burned Buffalo in retaliation and eventually burned Washington, D.C., as well. Meanwhile, villages across Upper Canada were the target of American attacks. In May, a group of invaders struck a series of small Lake Erie communities, setting fire to mills, shops, and houses before withdrawing. Those who escaped American attacks were nevertheless affected, always fearful that their homes might be next.

By this time, the government had grown weary of the American sympathizers among the general population. Orders were issued to round up suspected traitors. In May, a show trial was held in Ancaster. Fifteen men were found guilty of treason and eight were hanged at Burlington Heights. The executions sparked retaliation — one of the Crown witnesses was murdered a short time later at his home in Walpole Township, just west of the Grand River. The "Bloody Assize" sent a strong message about loyalty to the civilians of Upper Canada. Now, adding to the stresses of war was the worry that whatever a person did or said might be misinterpreted and reported to authorities.

As spring flowed into summer, conditions went from bad to worse. On July 3, the Americans captured Fort Erie. On July 5, they attacked Chippawa. About 6000 Americans gathered a few kilometres south of the village. General Phineas Riall, the British commander, assumed that most of them were volunteers who would retreat when faced with a direct attack. He was wrong. The men serving under U.S. General Winfield Scott were, in the words of historian Donald Graves, "the best trained unit in the American Army." They stood their ground. In the brief, bloody battle that followed, 415 men on the British side were killed, wounded, or missing, compared to 328 on the American side.

William Hamilton Merritt, who reached Chippawa that evening, recorded his impressions. "Every house was filled with the wounded. I stopped at Street's, and spent a very unpleasant night; many of the officers were lying wounded, groaning in pain." The young militia officer was furious that Riall had neither waited for reinforcements nor made use of the militia.

In the aftermath, the British force retreated to Burlington Heights, leaving the Niagara Peninsula again under the control of the Americans. Laura, who had probably heard the sound of the battle in Queenston, must have thanked God that her husband's injuries kept him from active service and that her son, Charles, was too young to join the militia. But this was a small comfort in the face of the American occupation. On July 19, the enemy burned the village of St. David's. Laura's brother-in-law, David Secord, was among those who lost nearly everything they owned that day. He would later ask the government to compensate him for those losses, including a three-storey frame house with seven fireplaces, two other stone houses, a gristmill, blacksmith shop, a new frame barn, and two log buildings, plus livestock, grain, family furnishings, clothing, and 1000 pounds of candles, which he had made under contract for British troops. The candles alone were valued at £100, more than many men earned in a year.

The Secords were still recovering from David's loss when the Americans and British clashed again, this time at Lundy's Lane. The battle was fought on a hot, dark night by exhausted troops who could barely tell who they were fighting. Casualties were heavy on both sides, but this time the British forced the Americans to retreat to Fort Erie.

On the night of August 14, Lieutenant General Gordon Drummond, the new commander of Upper Canada, attacked Fort Erie. Many British and Canadians were injured and killed, and they failed to oust the Americans from the fort. However, in the ensuing weeks, the British managed to maintain an uneasy stalemate. Finally, on November 5, the Americans withdrew. They would not return. On Christmas Eve 1814, the Treaty of Ghent was signed in Europe, ending the War of 1812.

The news took weeks to reach North America. In February, the *York Gazette* reported, "We hasten to perform the most grateful tasks ever imposed upon us, in the whole of our editorial labours. If the following intelligence shall be finally realized, in the completion of an Honorable Peace, the Country may rejoice." The report went on to explain that documents relating to the peace treaty had left England for the United States on January 2. Once they were ratified, the war in North America would officially come to an end.

Two and a half years of fighting had left thousands of dead and wounded and hundreds of buildings destroyed. In the end, neither side made significant gains. Laura and

James, like so many others, had paid a devastating price in pain, suffering, and loss. Now they had to try to pick up the pieces of their lives.

At the beginning of the war, James and Laura Secord had been reasonably well-off. Although financial problems were a constant worry, they had amassed some property and James's business was doing quite well. They had a comfortable house. By the end of the war, their house had been plundered twice and many of their personal possessions stolen or damaged by the enemy. James would never walk properly again, and the shoulder injury troubled him from time to time. Although, like so many other pioneers, he had the stamina and determination to keep going, his career as a merchant was over. His brother-in-law Richard Cartwright, who might have helped him get back on his feet, died in 1815. His brother David was still struggling with his own wartime losses. In 1817, James was forced to sell six lots he owned in Queenston in order to support Laura and the rest of the family, which by this time had expanded to seven children with the arrival of two more daughters, Laura, born in 1815, and Hannah, who arrived about a year later.

Like so many others affected by the war, James sent petitions to the government, asking for compensation for his losses and financial assistance. Following the standard formula that had been used in the aftermath of the American Revolution, most of the petitions stressed his loyalty and that of his family.

Unsung Heroine

On February 25, 1820, he asked Lieutenant-Governor Peregrine Maitland for permission to quarry stone in the Queenston military reserve. In doing so, he recounted his experiences during the war, as well as those of his wife:

The Petition of James Secord, Senior, of the Village of Queenston, Esquire, Humbly Sheweth

That your Petitioner is one of the oldest inhabitants of this Province — has had numerous Relatives in the British army, is Brother-in-Law to the late Honorable Richard Cartwright — is a Captain in the 2nd Regiment of Lincoln Militia — was wounded in the battle of Queenston — and twice plundered of all his Moveable property. That his wife embraced an opportunity of rendering some service, at the risk of her life, in going thro the Enemies' Lines to communicate information to a Detachment of His Majesty's Troops at Beaver Dam in the month of June 1813.

This was probably the first time Laura's walk to Beaver Dams was mentioned in an official document.

Peregrine Maitland was a career soldier who fought at the Battle of Waterloo and was knighted for his wartime service. While serving with the occupying forces in Paris after

Napoleon's defeat, the 38-year-old widower eloped with Lady Sarah Lennox, the 23-year-old daughter of the Duke of Richmond. The difference in their ages and social status infuriated his new father-in-law, but Richmond eventually came around through the intervention of the Duke of Wellington. When Richmond became governor-in-chief of British North America in 1818, Maitland was appointed lieutenant-governor of Upper Canada.

Maitland's unassuming and pleasant manner initially made him popular, and he worked diligently to fulfill his official duties. But he deeply disliked "Muddy York," much preferring the Niagara Peninsula. He and his wife built a lovely 22-room summer house, Stamford Park, five kilometres west of Niagara Falls. According to writer and traveller Anna Jameson, it was "an elegant, well-furnished English villa."

During his time in the Niagara area, Maitland became friendly with members of the Secord family. James was given permission to quarry rock, but whatever he earned from that enterprise was not enough to compensate him for his wartime losses. In another letter to the government, he reported that the Niagara District sheriff had confiscated all his property, probably in payment of outstanding debts. As a result, James wrote, "There is now no remedy for me but to be thrown upon the world penniless, lame and in ill health." While James may have been exaggerating his situation somewhat, the Secords' financial problems certainly would have caused Laura much worry.

In 1822, James again applied for assistance, citing his war injuries. The provincial medical board reported that he was "incapable of earning his livelihood in consequence of wounds received in action with the Enemy." He was awarded a small pension of £18 per year. Elsewhere, something was going on that might have helped improve the family finances.

Long before the War of 1812 ended, plans for a monument commemorating Isaac Brock were proceeding in England. On July 20, 1813, the British Parliament had passed a bill authorizing the construction of a memorial. Located in St. Paul's Cathedral in London, the monument depicts Brock, cradled in death by a British soldier, while a Native warrior stands watching them.

The people of Upper Canada were a little slower in honouring their fallen hero. In March 1814, Robert Nichol suggested that Upper Canadians commemorate Brock's "great and brilliant services" with a suitable monument. Nichol, a Scottish-born merchant, had worked closely with Brock in his capacity as quartermaster general for the province. In March 1815, the legislature passed an act to allow for the creation of a monument in Brock's memory. Lieutenant-Governor Sir Gordon Drummond, himself a veteran of the war, said it was his "unspeakable pleasure to assent to this act." The monument was to be built near the spot where Brock was killed. To finance the project, the legislature provided a sum of £500.

Eventually, a monument committee was appointed made up of Thomas Clark, Thomas Dickson, and Robert

Nichol, all of them veterans of the war. By this time, supporters of the scheme realized that the money initially earmarked for the monument was inadequate. The government agreed, voting another £1000 to complete the project.

Calls for tender finally appeared in colonial newspapers in the fall of 1823. The limestone monument would be "a Tower of cut-stone fifty feet [15 metres] in height and sixteen feet [5 metres] in diameter at the base with a winding stone stair inside and a vault underneath." In addition to the vault, the monument was designed with a square room in the base that functioned as a lobby for visitors. The spiral staircase led to an observation deck that gave a magnificent view of the countryside below.

Construction began the following spring. On June 1, 1824, the cornerstone was laid in a Masonic ceremony. William Lyon Mackenzie, who had recently opened his newspaper office in Queenston, was involved in the ceremony and had been asked to provide some of the items for a time capsule to be placed in the cornerstone. Among other items, the future rebel leader selected an issue of his newspaper that contained a report critical of Sir Peregrine Maitland. When Maitland heard about this, he ordered the cornerstone dug up and the offending copy of the *Colonial Advocate* removed.

The monument was dedicated on October 13, 1824, the 12th anniversary of Brock's death. Hundreds of people gathered at Fort George, where the bodies of Brock and

Macdonell were disinterred, placed in a black-draped hearse, and drawn by four black horses towards the site of the monument. Lining the route were members of the Lincoln militia, James Secord's former brothers-in-arms. In addition to a number of dignitaries, those following the bodies included chiefs of the Six Nations. Altogether, about 1500 people made up the cortege, which took three hours to cover the 11 kilometres to Queenston. By the time they arrived, several thousand people had converged at the site of the monument. The bodies were laid to rest with appropriate pomp and ceremony, then covered with stone slabs.

As construction continued over the next few years, there was some discussion about who would take care of the monument. Knowing the Secords' precarious financial situation, as well as the loyalty demonstrated by their wartime service, Sir Peregrine Maitland suggested that Laura be given the position of caretaker once the monument was completed. Her duties would include collecting admission fees from visitors and, presumably, providing refreshments from the bar. Laura initially refused the offer, but she later changed her mind.

In 1828, James was appointed registrar of the Niagara District Surrogate Court. The position brought some prestige and a little money, but not much. Writing to Laura's sister Mira Hutchinson in December 1829, James said, "We are not very prosperous. We make out to live and have clothing and food, but riches, my dear woman, it seems to me, is not for

James Secord." James also took time to report on the family's health, telling Mira, "Your sister Laura never had health better. She bears her age most remarkably considering her former delicate state of body."

Although there are occasional references to Laura's delicate health, no records exist that provide further information. James FitzGibbon had described her as a delicate-looking woman. Laura herself made passing reference to an ailment that began as a result of her walk to FitzGibbon's headquarters. There are no details. Yet Laura had given birth to seven children, all of whom lived to adulthood. She had also survived Elizabeth Secord, the niece who had accompanied her during part of the walk to Beaver Dams. Elizabeth died in 1814, before she could marry Laura's half-brother Charles. Some time later Charles married Anna Maria Merritt, the sister of his friend William Hamilton Merritt. While Laura may have suffered from some chronic ailment, her overall health seems to have been good.

Some months before James wrote his letter to Mira, Laura and a group of visiting relatives toured Brock's monument, signing their names in the visitors' book. By this time, it was one of the most famous tourist attractions in Canada. Everyone who could afford the trip made their way to Niagara Falls. Once there, it was a short distance to Brock's monument, where visitors could gaze in awe at the spectacular landscape or reflect on the glorious sacrifice Isaac Brock had made at the Battle of Queenston Heights. There must have been a caretaker on the premises at this point, but perhaps he or she resigned soon afterwards. In any event, Laura apparently expected to take on the job.

Certain individuals in government had other ideas. The three commissioners who had been appointed to oversee the construction and operation of the monument were part of an extensive network of prominent businessmen and office-holders. All three were born in Scotland, probably in the same area. Thomas Dickson and Thomas Clark were cousins. Along with Robert Nichol, they worked for Robert Hamilton, the wealthy merchant in whose garden Isaac Brock had waited before his fatal attempt to retake the redan gun at the Battle of Queenston Heights. All three served in the militia.

Dickson had received a minor wound at the Battle of Chippawa. Clark had fought at Queenston Heights and been among the reinforcements who arrived in time to witness the Americans' surrender to James FitzGibbon at Beaver Dams. Robert Nichol, whom FitzGibbon once described as "a mean looking little Scotchman, who squinted very much," wrote an extremely useful report on the men, horses, and provisions available in Upper Canada at the outset of the war. As quartermaster general, he was in charge of the movement of supplies throughout the province. In all likelihood, Laura and James Secord knew all three men reasonably well, either because of common business interests or wartime activity. In addition, once the war ended Thomas Dickson worked with the Loyal and Patriotic Society of Canada to distribute money to those in need because of war losses.

By 1829, however, two of the commissioners were long dead. Dickson's health had never been particularly good, and he died in January 1825. Nichol had died the previous May in a spectacular accident. On the night of May 3, 1824, as he was returning to Queenston after official business, his horse and wagon plunged over the escarpment near Queenston Heights. Nichol was smashed to death on the rocks.

With Nichol and Dickson gone, Clark was the last surviving commissioner. Although he had lost his mills to the enemy during the war, he had recovered financially. In fact, he was one of the wealthiest men in Upper Canada and owned a 40-room house overlooking Niagara Falls. In his opinion, the person who should be appointed caretaker at Brock's monument was Theresa Nichol. She and Robert had been married just over 12 years at the time of his death and had four young children. Although Nichol's estate was awarded more than £4000 in compensation for war losses, the family was still struggling to survive.

Clark urged the government to appoint Theresa Nichol to the caretaker's job. According to Laura, Lieutenant-Governor Maitland told him "it was too late to think of Mrs. Nichol as I had pledged my word to Mrs. Secord that as soon as possible she should have the *key*." A note scribbled on one of James's petitions by John Beverley Robinson, later chief justice of the province, stated that Maitland "had a favourable opinion of the character & claims of Mr. Secord and his wife." He also stated that Clark mentioned several times the suggestion that Laura should be appointed caretaker. According to Robinson, Clark "seemed disappointed that the offer shd. have been made to Mrs. Secord, as he had in his own mind intended to have proposed Mrs. Nichol." When Maitland left the province in 1828, Sir John Colborne replaced him as lieutenant-governor. Colborne had no connection with the Secords, and in 1831 Theresa Nichol was appointed caretaker of the monument.

Laura was furious and wrote an angry letter to Colborne's secretary. It may have relieved some of her tension, but it did nothing to change the situation. Another caretaker was in charge, and every time she saw the monument, Laura must have thought of her disappointment.

Chapter 6
Recognition

n spite of the disappointment about Brock's monument, the Secords were making some headway in their struggle for financial security. In 1833, James was promoted, becoming a judge of the Niagara District Surrogate Court. Charles Secord, James and Laura's son, replaced James as registrar. Two years later, James moved to another, more lucrative position, that of collector of customs at Chippawa. There was no salary attached to the job. Instead, the collector was allowed to keep a percentage of the fees collected for goods passing through the port, as well as a share of any smuggled goods that he seized. Most years, James earned well over £100, more than five times what he received from his war pension.

By this time the Welland Canal had been built. The

waterway, designed to provide a shortcut around Niagara Falls for boats travelling between Lakes Ontario and Erie, was the brainchild of William Hamilton Merritt. Although the route would later divert traffic to Welland and St. Catharines, in the early years Chippawa remained an important port along the canal and the town prospered. It was during this period that James Secord was collector of customs.

The job brought with it a certain number of hazards. Smugglers sometimes tried to get shipments past customs without duty. On one occasion, James was told that an attempt would be made on a particular night. He had one man he could count on to assist him in dealing with the smugglers, but he thought he might have a better chance at persuading them to give up their goods if a third man was present. Time was short, so Laura dressed herself in James's coat and trousers and posed as the third man. It was highly unusual for a respectable woman to dress in men's clothing, but Laura, as always, was ready to help James. Certainly there was some risk, but if she lurked in the background, there was a good chance the smugglers would find her menacing and give in to James's demands. Apparently the plan worked perfectly.

In early December 1837, rebellion broke out in Upper Canada. The leader was none other than William Lyon Mackenzie, the fiery politician who had once published a newspaper in Queenston. When the uprising was quickly suppressed by government troops, many of the rebels fled to the United

States. Mackenzie retreated to Navy Island, directly opposite Chippawa, where he set up a provisional government. Over the next several weeks, he was joined by dozens of followers. The men lived in makeshift wooden shacks, just beyond the reach of Upper Canadian authorities, plotting their next moves. Supplies were brought to them by the American steamer *Caroline*, which was based at Fort Schlosser.

Loyal colonists were deeply insulted by the presence of rebels so close to Canadian waters. It was not long before they struck at them. On the night of December 29, Commander Andrew Drew of the Royal Navy led a group of Canadian militiamen to Fort Schlosser. After a brief fight in which one American was killed, the *Caroline* was cut loose, set afire, and then allowed to drift along the river until she was swept over Niagara Falls. Samuel Strickland, young brother of pioneer writers Catharine Parr Traill and Susanna Moodie, described the scene, which many others living close to the river would have witnessed. "The night was intensely dark, yet every surrounding object was distinctly visible in the wild glare caused by the *Caroline* as she rushed into the thundering abyss below." The attack on a boat in American waters strained the uneasy relations between British North America and the United States. However, on January 5, U.S. president Martin Van Buren formally declared his country neutral in the matter of the Canadian rebellion. Nine days later, heavy British artillery fire forced the rebels off the island.

The rebel threat had not ended, however. Over the

next few years there were a number of attacks on Canadian targets. In June 1838, a group of rebels crossed over from the United States and spent 10 days terrorizing the Short Hills area, south of St. Catharines, before they were rounded up. In November, two men called at the Chippawa home of Captain Edgeworth Ussher, the man who had piloted the boats in the attack on the *Caroline*. Although it was close to one in the morning, Ussher answered his door and was immediately shot dead.

On April 17, 1840, someone placed gunpowder at the base of Brock's monument and tried to blow it up. The explosion damaged the structure so badly that it had to be demolished. The bodies of Brock and Macdonell were removed from the vault and reinterred in the Hamilton family cemetery at Queenston. It took several years of discussion, but on October 13, 1853, building began on a new monument. It was completed in the fall of 1856.

For Laura and James Secord, the incursions by rebels were grim reminders of the events of the War of 1812. Again, there was the constant fear of attack, the worries about personal injury and loss of property. And, again, there was the atmosphere of suspicion that turned citizens against one another. This time, even James could not escape the paranoia of the period, which manifested itself in a resurgence of anti-American feeling. At one point, James was accused of anti-government sentiments because his deputy customs collector was not a British citizen. Perhaps the fact that both

The Laura Secord home, Chippawa, Ontario

he and Laura had been born in the United States was mentioned as well. James defended himself in a letter written to Sir George Arthur on August 29, 1840, noting that he had lived in Upper Canada for more than 60 years, had fought in the War of 1812, and that "gentlemen of the first standing in Toronto & elsewhere" could be consulted to vouch for his "Honour, Integrity & Loyalty." Although the attempt at character assassination was probably not taken seriously by anyone who knew the Secords well, it must have created some bitter feeling for the couple who had spent their adult lives wholly committed to the British flag.

Financial problems continued to plague James and

Laura in old age. Their family was grown, although, tragically, Appollonia died at the age of 18. She had been the baby of the family when Laura brought her warning to James FitzGibbon. Many pioneer women lost children to sickness or accidents, but Laura had been singularly lucky with her own family. The death of Appollonia, just as she reached young womanhood, came as a bitter blow.

Charles had married, as had all of his surviving sisters except Charlotte, who remained single throughout her life. Mary married William Trumble, a military surgeon, in 1816 and moved to Ireland with him. When he died in the late 1820s, he left her an estate and a good pension. Harriet, Laura, and Hannah were also widowed after several years of marriage, but they were apparently not as well off as Mary. Following the deaths of their husbands, they moved back to their parents' home. Although they all eventually remarried, Laura and James were again responsible for their daughters' support for long periods of time.

Once more Laura turned to petitions to try to increase the family income. In early 1840, she wrote to the lieutenant-governor, asking for the concession to run the ferry between Queenston and Lewiston. The petition revealed the family's precarious financial situation. In it Laura stressed that, while she would not "presume" to ask for remuneration, she was forced to do so "from the circumstances of having a large family of Daughters & Grand Daughters to provide for & for which the small means of my Husband Captain James Secord

Sen'r will not meet." She included a description of her 1813 adventure, as well as a certificate supporting her statement, written by James FitzGibbon.

Laura waited anxiously for a response as she went about her daily tasks. The petition was never far from her mind. A positive response from the government would make life just a little more comfortable for her family. In addition, the official recognition that came with a government appointment would increase the Secords' status in the community, making it clear that they were well regarded by those in power. But the government ignored the request.

The following year, Laura submitted more petitions. This time, there was an extra urgency about them. On February 22, 1841, James Secord died. At his request, he was laid to rest in the Drummond Hill cemetery, near other veterans of the War of 1812. Laura, widowed at 64 after more than 40 years of marriage, pushed aside her grief to look after the immediate needs of the family. One of her first actions was to petition the government to make Charles his father's successor as collector of customs. This request was rejected, quite likely because of changes in the provincial government. Just 12 days before James Secord died, the Act of Union went into effect, uniting Canada East (formerly Lower Canada) and Canada West (Upper Canada) in the United Province of Canada. Meanwhile, the new governor general, Lord Sydenham, tried to implement reforms that would make the government of the united provinces run more smoothly while doing away with the worst aspects of patronage.

Laura also submitted a petition in 1841 requesting a pension. She stressed that she was "far advanced in years and consequently ... unable to make much exertion for her own maintenance." The small war pension James had been granted had ceased with his death.

Again, the government turned a deaf ear. Somehow, Laura managed, possibly with the help of her family. Towards the end of 1841, she left the house that she and James had shared and bought a red brick cottage for £155. For a short time she kept a private school there, probably teaching a few local children the basics of "reading, 'riting, and 'rithmetic." This was a means by which many women in the colonial period eked out a small living, charging parents a fee for teaching their children. But the times were changing. In September 1841, the Common Schools Act passed, guaranteeing an elementary education for the children of Canada. For the first time, part of the funding would come from the government. The new legislation, as well as Laura's advancing years, quickly ended her teaching career.

By this time, the War of 1812 was far enough in the past for the worst of it to have been forgotten. It had become a dramatic part of Canadian history, a pivotal point that shaped the destiny and character of Upper Canada. As participants aged, stories about their adventures and their bravery were recorded, and some of them were published in the magazines and newspapers that were starting to pop up across the province.

Detail of *Laura Secord,* painting by Mildred Peel

Laura may have told her story on a number of occa-
sions, both to her family and friends. According to family tradition, she was a gregarious, outgoing woman who was well
liked by younger people, and so her story may have been one
of those local tales that everyone knew but nobody thought

about too deeply. Then, in 1845, Laura's son Charles wrote about her famous walk in a letter to an Anglican paper, *The Church*. This was the first step in bringing the story of Laura's part in the Battle of Beaver Dams to a wider audience. Still, the story might have been forgotten as time passed had it not been for the involvement of one very prominent person.

In 1860, Albert Edward, Prince of Wales and eldest son of Queen Victoria, toured Canada. Long before he left England, Canadian newspapers were providing minute details about the prince and his imminent visit. One report included this description: "The prince stands five feet six inches in height, is slender in form, having a narrow head, intelligent face, large, handsome eyes, small mouth, a large nose, receding chin, complexion rather dark, boyish appearance, and generally resembling his mother at about the time of her coronation. He has rather large hands and feet, is very graceful in his movements, unostentatious and affable. He talks a good deal: and in a rather loud and somewhat harsh tone of voice. His ordinary costume is that of a colonel of the British army."

Everything the prince did was watched and reported on, whether it was placing the last rivet in Montreal's Victoria Bridge or laying the cornerstone of the new Parliament buildings in Ottawa. Today, most arrangements for royal tours are made months in advance. In 1860, however, many of the details were left until the last minute. So, as the prince made his way across the country, the most influential citizens of various towns competed for his attention, doing their best to persuade the royal entourage to stop in their community.

Like most tourists, the prince had to see Niagara Falls. It was also politically wise to acknowledge the contributions that loyal Canadians had made in the War of 1812 and the Rebellions of 1837. So, early on, arrangements were made for several stops in the Niagara Peninsula. The first was at the village of Chippawa, and Laura was probably in the crowd that watched the prince arrive.

The prince was on his way back from the western parts of the province. After the royal train reached Fort Erie, he and his party transferred to the steamer *Clifton* and chugged up the Niagara River. They arrived after dark to find a red carpet waiting for them at Macklem's dock and the whole area illuminated by torches. The crowd gave three cheers as the prince stepped ashore and raised his hat in acknowledgement of their greeting. Then he climbed into a waiting carriage and, followed by several other vehicles and pedestrians, slowly made his way to the Pavilion Hotel. After the requisite speeches, he was whisked off to a private home.

During his visit, the prince spent some time gazing at the falls. He also witnessed a stunning performance by Blondin, the most celebrated tightrope walker of the day. On Sunday, he went to services at Holy Trinity Church, the same church Laura attended. A number of people were presented to the prince during his visit, but whether Laura was introduced to the royal visitor at this time is unknown. What is known is that she prepared a document that she hoped to give him. Just as she had done in her petitions, Laura stressed her loyalty and asked that the prince convey to his "Royal Parent the Queen" the "name of one who in the hour of trial and danger ... stood ever ready and willing to defend this Country against every invasion come what might." Again she attached James FitzGibbon's certificate describing her walk to DeCew's house, but this time she added something extra, a statement written by Welland County Warden James Cummings: "I Certify that I have for many years, been personally acquainted with Mrs. Secord named in the above Certificate; and that she is the person she represents herself to be in her Memorial hereunto annexed. And further she is a person of the most Respectable Character."

On Tuesday, September 18, the prince was in Queenston. For many people in the area, this was the highlight of his visit because the day's events included a ceremony in which the prince paid tribute to Isaac Brock and the veterans of the War of 1812. Some time earlier, the veterans had decided they would present a signed address to the prince. Any veterans who cared to sign had simply to drop into the office of the Clerk of the Peace at Niagara. Among those who called at the office was Laura Secord. At first the astonished clerk refused to allow her to sign. But Laura, determined as always, insisted. Perhaps she showed him FitzGibbon's certificate. At any rate, she was allowed to sign and when the address was handed to the prince, someone pointed out Laura's name. With his curiosity aroused, the prince asked a number of questions. After his return to England, he arranged for an award of £100 in gold to be sent to Laura. It was the only financial compensation she would ever receive for her part in the War of 1812.

By now, Laura was very elderly, but still alert and interested in the goings-on around her. Benson Lossing, an American historian, visited her in 1867, when he was researching his book on the War of 1812. He gives us a glimpse of the older Laura: "She is now living at the Canadian village of Chippewa, on the Niagara River, at the age of ninety-two years, her mental faculties in full play, and her eyesight sufficiently retained to see to read without spectacles."

Laura died in 1868 and was buried beside James in Drummond Hill cemetery. Her obituary in the *Niagara Mail* retold the story of her walk to Beaver Dams, recognizing her as "one of the Canadian women of the war of 1812, whose spirit and devotion to their country contributed so much to its defence."

Epilogue

In typical mid-Victorian fashion, the first books about the War of 1812 gave the leading roles to men. In 1853, when Gilbert Auchinleck published a history of the war in the *Anglo-American Magazine*, Laura's story appeared in a footnote. Similarly, when American historian Benson J. Lossing wrote *The Pictorial Field-Book of the War of 1812* in the 1860s, his emphasis was on men's involvement.

By this time, Laura was becoming better known, but early biographers were not always careful with the facts. Their main interest was in publicizing Laura Secord as a celebrity, a genuine heroine who had helped save Upper Canada from American invaders during one of the darkest chapters of its history. Frequently they downplayed her late-Loyalist origins, preferring to hide the fact that her father had fought on the wrong side during the American Revolution.

Early writers also added all kinds of fictional details to Laura's story. W.F. Coffin, who published *War of 1812 and its Moral* in 1864, introduced a cow that he said Laura brought along to convince American sentries she was only interested in her farm chores. That cow was pure invention, but it caught people's imagination and still comes up whenever Laura Secord is discussed. Other writers claimed she made the walk in bare feet or that she fainted on arriving at FitzGibbon's headquarters.

Nearly 90 years after the Battle of Beaver Dams, in 1901, the first public monument to Laura Secord was unveiled at the Drummond Hill cemetery. In 1911, a granite memorial, almost four metres tall, was dedicated at Queenston Heights, not far from Brock's monument.

Further recognition of Laura's status as a Canadian icon came in 1913, when Frank O'Connor opened a chain of candy stores named after her. The Toronto senator wanted a name that would evoke Canadian tradition and wholesomeness.

By the 1930s, Laura Secord was a name familiar to generations of Canadians. So when historian William Stewart Wallace suggested Laura's account was full of holes and that she had contributed nothing to the victory at Beaver Dams, a controversy erupted. He based his arguments on three main points. First, Laura was conspicuously absent from most contemporary accounts of the Battle of Beaver Dams. Second, her claim that she walked 31 or 32 kilometres was inaccurate, since the distance from Queenston to DeCew's house was closer to 19 kilometres. Finally, the information in the documents Wallace discussed suggested that Laura arrived *after* FitzGibbon had learned of American movements from Native scouts. In Wallace's opinion, the Secords had concocted the story of Laura's attempt to warn FitzGibbon in order to strengthen their post-war demands for money and position.

Epilogue

Wallace's arguments convinced some people and outraged many others. Henry Cartwright Secord, a descendant of Laura's brother-in-law Stephen Secord, went a long way towards refuting Wallace's arguments when he produced a certificate written by James FitzGibbon in 1820. The certificate was useful historical evidence, but what really undermined Wallace's argument was the fact that he had been completely unaware of it, even though it was stored in the Archives of Ontario. Henry Secord's find suggested Wallace had not done his homework.

Wallace backed down a little. In an encyclopedia he edited in the late 1930s, he described Laura as a heroine, but made no assessment of the value and timeliness of the message she relayed to FitzGibbon.

In 1959, historian John S. Moir re-examined Wallace's arguments in light of the discovery of another certificate written by James FitzGibbon. The new document settled "the problem of the date of Mrs. Secord's walk, of the success of her mission, and perhaps throws a more charitable light on the motives of the Secords in their recurrent pleas to the government for pecuniary relief." Moir quoted the document at the end of his article. Written by James FitzGibbon at York on May 11, 1827, it stated that Laura had reached DeCew's house on June 22 "after Sun Set." According to FitzGibbon, it was James who had heard the details of the forthcoming attack, which was scheduled for the morning of June 23. FitzGibbon continued: "In consequence of this information I placed the

Indians under Norton together with my own Detachment in a Situation to intercept the American Detachment, and we occupied it during the night of the 22nd. — but the Enemy did not come until the morning of the 24th when his Detachment was captured. Captain Boerstler, their commander, in a conversation with me confirmed fully the information communicated to me by Mrs. Secord, and accounted for the attempt not having been made on the 23rd as at first intended."

FitzGibbon also expressed his appreciation of Laura's action, especially in view of the physical effort involved. "I have ever since held myself personally indebted to her for her conduct upon that occasion, and I consider it an imperative duty on my part humbly and earnestly to recommend her to the favourable consideration of His Majesty's Provincial Government."

The chocolate company is probably the first thing that comes to mind when people hear the name Laura Secord. But many, if pressed a little, can come up with some of the details of her journey. She has burrowed her way into our collective conscience in a way that few historical figures have done. How this came about is clearly stated on the plaque at her home in Queenston. "Her courage, tenacity, and patriotism have made her Ontario's best-known heroine."

Acknowledgments

Quoted material that appears in this book comes from many sources. The author gratefully acknowledges the following: Elizabeth Abbott, editor. *Chronicle of Canada*. Montreal: Chronicle Publications, 1990; *Dictionary of Canadian Biography; Erie News* (Norfolk County, Ontario); Benson J. Lossing, *The Pictorial Field-Book of the War of 1812*. Glendale, New York: Benchmark Publishing Corporation 1970 (original published 1869); Robert Malcomson, *Burying General Brock: A History of Brock's Monuments*. Niagara-on-the-Lake: The Friends of Fort George, 1996; Ruth McKenzie, *Laura Secord: The Lady and the Legend*. Toronto: McClelland and Stewart Limited, 1971, and *James FitzGibbon, Defender of Upper Canada*. Toronto: Dundurn Press, 1983. John S. Moir, "An Early Record of Laura Secord's Walk" in *Ontario History* Volume LI (1959) No. 2, 105–108; and Jack Williams, *Merritt: A Canadian Before His Time*. St. Catharines: Stonehouse Publications, 1985.

Thanks also go to McMaster University Library, the archives at Haldimand County Museum (Cayuga) and Eva Brook Donly Museum (Simcoe), and to my editor, Yvonne Van Ruskenveld, whose patience and skill resulted in significant improvements to this book.

About the Author

Cheryl MacDonald has been writing about Canadian history for nearly 30 years. A long-time resident of Nanticoke, Ontario, she is a full-time writer and historian whose weekly history column appears in the *Simcoe Times-Reformer.* Her historical articles have appeared in *The Beaver, Maclean's, Hamilton Spectator,* and *The Old Farmer's Almanac.* Cheryl has written more than 20 books on the history of Ontario and Canada, including the Amazing Stories titles *Niagara Daredevils, Great Canadian Love Stories,* and *Christmas in Ontario.* Currently completing a master's degree in history at McMaster University in Hamilton, she can be contacted through her website: www.heronwoodent.ca

Further Reading

Malcomson, Robert. *Burying General Brock: A History of Brock's Monuments*. Niagara-on-the-Lake: The Friends of Fort George, 1996.

McKenzie, Ruth. *James FitzGibbon, Defender of Upper Canada*. Toronto: Dundurn Press, 1983.

McKenzie, Ruth. *Laura Secord: The Lady and the Legend*. Toronto: McClelland and Stewart Limited, 1971.

Amazing Author
Question and Answer

What surprised you most while you were conducting you research for this Amazing Story?

The relatively small amount of solid information about Laura Secord, her famous walk, and her family. There are many, many legends, but comparatively little that can be verified.

What difficulties did you run into while researching the book?

Sorting out fact from fiction and steering clear of academic controversy. It seems that every 20 or 30 years since the 1880s Laura's story has been revised.

What do you most admire about Laura Secord?

Persistence. Laura could have given up at any time during her walk; she could have given up her quest for recognition at any time during her life, but she kept on trying.

What part of the writing process did you enjoy most?

Being able to weave in the actual words of the people in the story, using what letters and documents survive.

Why did you become a writer? Who inspired you?

I was an avid reader by the time I was eight years old. I can't say any one person inspired me (except perhaps poet Irving Layton, who wrote a lovely, encouraging note after my mother sent him a bunch of my TERRIBLE poems.) Probably I was more inspired by the idea that you could actually write for a living.

What is your next project?

I have just completed *Deadly Women of Ontario* for the Amazing Stories series. I'm also researching the history of gunboats manned by British sailors that patrolled the Great Lakes from 1866–1868.

Who are your Canadian heroes?

There are too many to list here, but they include William Van Horne, Nellie McClung, Emily Carr, Adelaide Hoodless, Tom Longboat, J.S. Woodsworth, Tommy Douglas, Egerton Ryerson, and Abigail Becker.

Which other Amazing Stories would you recommend?

War of 1812 and *Life of a Loyalist* for anyone interested in the background to Laura Secord's story.

Amazing Places to Visit

The Niagara Peninsula has many tourist attractions connected with the War of 1812 and early settlers, including:

Brock's Monument, Queenston (Niagara-on-the-Lake)

Fort George National Historic Site, Niagara-on-the-Lake.
www.parkscanada.gc.ca

Laura Secord Homestead, Niagara Falls
www.niagaraparks.com

by the same author

AMAZING STORIES™

GREAT CANADIAN LOVE STORIES

Romances, Affairs, and Passionate Tales

ROMANCE/HISTORY
by Cheryl MacDonald

ISBN 1-55153-973-X

by the same author

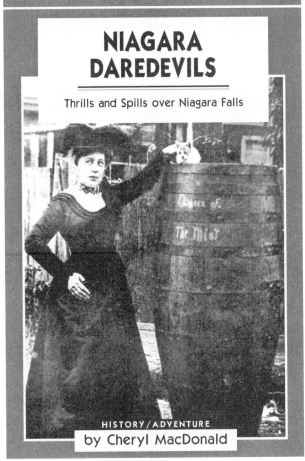

AMAZING STORIES™

NIAGARA DAREDEVILS

Thrills and Spills over Niagara Falls

HISTORY/ADVENTURE
by Cheryl MacDonald

ISBN 1-55153-962-4

AMAZING STORIES

by the same author

AMAZING STORIES™

CHRISTMAS IN ONTARIO

Heartwarming Legends, Tales, and Traditions

HOLIDAY

by Cheryl MacDonald

ISBN 1-55153-779-6

OTHER AMAZING STORIES

ISBN	Title	ISBN	Title
1-55153-959-4	A War Bride's Story	1-55153-951-9	Ontario Murders
1-55153-794-X	Calgary Flames	1-55153-790-7	Ottawa Senators
1-55153-947-0	Canada's Rumrunners	1-55153-960-8	Ottawa Titans
1-55153-966-7	Canadian Spies	1-55153-945-4	Pierre Elliot Trudeau
1-55153-795-8	D-Day	1-55153-981-0	Rattenbury
1-55153-972-1	David Thompson	1-55153-991-8	Rebel Women
1-55153-982-9	Dinosaur Hunters	1-55153-995-0	Rescue Dogs
1-55153-970-5	Early Voyageurs	1-55153-985-3	Riding on the Wild Side
1-55153-798-2	Edmonton Oilers	1-55153-974-8	Risk Takers and Innovators
1-55153-968-3	Edwin Alonzo Boyd	1-55153-956-X	Robert Service
1-55153-996-9	Emily Carr	1-55153-799-0	Roberta Bondar
1-55153-961-6	Étienne Brûlé	1-55153-997-7	Sam Steele
1-55153-791-5	Extraordinary Accounts of Native Life on the West Coast	1-55153-954-3	Snowmobile Adventures
		1-55153-971-3	Stolen Horses
1-55153-992-6	Ghost Town Stories II	1-55153-952-7	Strange Events
1-55153-984-5	Ghost Town Stories III	1-55153-783-4	Strange Events and More
1-55153-993-4	Ghost Town Stories	1-55153-986-1	Tales from the West Coast
1-55153-973-X	Great Canadian Love Stories	1-55153-978-0	The Avro Arrow Story
		1-55153-943-8	The Black Donnellys
1-55153-777-X	Great Cat Stories	1-55153-942-X	The Halifax Explosion
1-55153-946-2	Great Dog Stories	1-55153-994-2	The Heart of a Horse
1-55153-773-7	Great Military Leaders	1-55153-944-6	The Life of a Loyalist
1-55153-785-0	Grey Owl	1-55153-787-7	The Mad Trapper
1-55153-958-6	Hudson's Bay Company Adventures	1-55153-789-3	The Mounties
		1-55153-948-9	The War of 1812 Against the States
1-55153-969-1	Klondike Joe Boyle		
1-55153-980-2	Legendary Show Jumpers	1-55153-788-5	Toronto Maple Leafs
1-55153-775-3	Lucy Maud Montgomery	1-55153-976-4	Trailblazing Sports Heroes
1-55153-967-5	Marie Anne Lagimodière		
1-55153-964-0	Marilyn Bell	1-55153-977-2	Unsung Heroes of the Royal Canadian Air Force
1-55153-999-3	Mary Schäffer		
1-55153-953-5	Moe Norman	1-55153-792-3	Vancouver Canucks
1-55153-965-9	Native Chiefs and Famous Métis	1-55153-989-6	Vancouver's Old-Time Scoundrels
		1-55153-990-X	West Coast Adventures
1-55153-962-4	Niagara Daredevils	1-55153-987-X	Wilderness Tales
1-55153-793-1	Norman Bethune	1-55153-873-3	Women Explorers

These titles are available wherever you buy books. If you have trouble finding the book you want, call the Altitude order desk at **1-800-957-6888**, e-mail your request to: **orderdesk@altitudepublishing.com** or visit our Web site **at www.amazingstories.ca**

New AMAZING STORIES titles are published every month.